WHODUNITS

WHODUNITS

Test your crime-solving skills with this engrossing collection

TIM DEDOPULOS

SIRIUS

SIRIUS

This edition published in 2024 by Sirius Publishing, a division of
Arcturus Publishing Limited,
26/27 Bickels Yard, 151–153 Bermondsey Street,
London SE1 3HA

ISBN: 978-1-3988-3672-3
AD010991NT

Printed in China

Contents

INTRODUCTION

The solving of puzzles is one of humanity's universal pastimes. Every culture we know of engages in recreational problem-solving, and archaeologists have found records and remains of puzzles right back to the earliest days of civilization. The application of intelligence to solve problems is the trait that led our species to where we are today, so it's no surprise that it's such a fundamental part of our existence.

It's a very good thing that it is, too. Recent scientific discoveries have confirmed what we have all long suspected: that "use it or lose it" applies just as much to mental fitness as it does

Miss Mary Miller

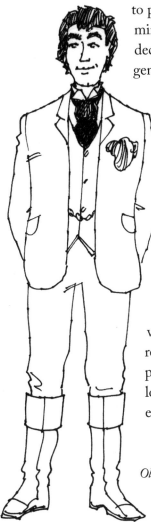

to physical strength. The more active the mind is kept, the smaller the risk of cognitive decline as we get older. Daily puzzle-solving genuinely helps to keep us in good shape!

The puzzles in this book are a little bit special. In each vignette, you will encounter a number of characters, and one or more of them will be attempting to deceive. Everything you need to identify the culprit is there for you on the page – an inconsistency, an impossibility or some tell-tale detail will reveal the guilty party. You have to find the flaw in the story and thus uncover the criminal.

In the first section, Level 1, the vignettes are quite short and the flaws reasonably straightforward. The Level 2 puzzles are a bit harder. The scenarios are longer, the evidence less clear, and the events more complicated. But there are

Oliver James

clues to help you if you need them, and also a few red herrings to keep you on your mettle.

Before we get to the puzzles I want to introduce you to our sleuths: Inspector Ignatius "Paddington" Parnacki, Miss Mary Miller and Oliver James. One of them will feature in each of our stories, and you will be "shadowing" them to get to the truth behind our cases.

Happy sleuthing!

Tim Dedopulos

Inspector "Paddington" Parnacki

CASES

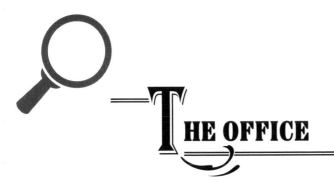

THE OFFICE

"**I** can't believe poor Victor is dead. I just had coffee with him not two hours ago." Dr. Rigg certainly seemed distressed. "He and I co-own this building, along with Owen Price on the second floor."

Inspector Parnacki nodded. "So I understand. I believe Mr. Floyd was a private investigator?"

"Yes. My practice is on the first floor, Owen has a law office on the second, and Victor's office is up top. We shared the mortgage payments equally between us. He never seemed to have any trouble keeping up his share."

"Did anyone?" asked Parnacki.

"Well, Owen has been having a rather tricky time recently, and I know he'd like us to sell this building so he could move somewhere cheaper. Victor and I had offered to let him reduce his share a little for a few months, though, until things picked up. I don't know what will happen now. How did he die, may I ask?"

"Our investigations are ongoing," Parnacki said.

The victim's receptionist, Megan Kane, knew exactly what had happened. "It was poison," she told Parnacki tearfully. "He and Dr. Rigg had just finished their morning coffees. Vic went into his room, and made a call. He got as far as 'Good morning', when he gasped and started wheezing horribly. He started to stagger towards my room. He looked terrible. Then he fell to his hands and knees, crawled a few paces, and … and … he died." She burst out weeping again.

Inspector Parnacki offered her a handkerchief, and gave her a few moments. Once she had recovered a little, he smiled at her encouragingly. "What happened then?"

"I screamed," Megan said. "Then I ran downstairs to find Dr. Rigg. He had gone out, but Suzanna, his assistant, called the police, and looked after me until you came. It … it must have been Dr. Rigg! They'd just had coffee. But why would he kill Vic? He seems so nice." She broke down again.

"Perhaps," said Parnacki gently. "Where was Mr. Price in all this?"

"Oh," she sniffled, "Mr. Price was here early, and I could hear that he was disagreeing with Vic about something. But then he left to go to meetings across town, so he's been gone for hours. No one else has

come by today."

"Thank you, Miss Kane. You've been a great help." Parnacki left the receptionist and went into the detective's office. The room was dominated by an untidy desk bearing an empty coffee mug, various papers, several file folders, a jug of water with a couple of glasses, a telephone on its stand, an inkwell and pens, and some sheets of blotting paper. Behind it was a comfortable chair and in front stood a pair of more formal chairs for visitors. Filing cabinets lined one wall, and bookshelves the other. The building's mortgage agreement was prominent amid the clutter on the desk.

Taking great care, the inspector cautiously sniffed the mug, noticing a faint, bitter hint of almond. Definitely poison, then.

He returned to the reception area and sat down next to Megan again. "I now know enough to bring the murderer to justice," he told her.

Who is it, and how does he know?
HINT:
DESK.

THE FOREMAN PIECES

"They knew just what they were looking for, Mary." Stella's eyebrows were knotted in irritation.

Miss Miller clucked sympathetically. "Would you like some more tea, my dear? What a horrible business this must be for you."

Stella Simmons pushed her cup and saucer over. "It is horrible, yes. That's a good word. Losing the pieces is annoying, but that's not the thing. One feels so … invaded."

It had been two days since the break-in. Three expensive Foreman statuettes had been seized, but nothing else.

"That does fade, I promise you," Miss Miller said. "It takes some time, though. You might want to hire some extra help to keep watch on things for a few weeks. Although I'm sure they won't be back. They got what they wanted. Foreman is very desirable at the moment, so there's quite a bit of his work on the market."

"Don't I know it," Stella said. "The police were quite pessimistic. Said it would be a devil of a chore to positively identify my pieces if they've already been sold on. Which, they think, they will have been."

"Have you had much trouble with the press?"

"Oh, them." Stella sighed. "Blasted idiots couldn't get anything right. Spelled Simmons with a 'd', claimed I'd lost five pieces, and utterly fabricated a supposed quote about how 'utterly distraught' I was to have lost 'priceless family heirlooms packed with memories'. Complete nonsense. I'm obviously not happy, but I got the damned things last winter because they were attractive."

"Any idea how they knew where to look?"

"Oh, I don't think they did. They went through several rooms downstairs, poking around. They only wanted the Foremans."

"I suppose it's no secret you liked his work."

"Not since I agreed to that dratted interview a few months ago, no. What the contents of my home has to do with migrating plovers, I have no idea."

"I think they call it scene-setting," Miss Miller said. She paused. "Oh, Aubrey, no, not on the table. It's just tea, sweetie." She picked her cat up from where he was nosing at her cup, and set him back down on the floor.

Stella managed a weak grin for the cat.

"I'm not promising anything," Miss Miller said. "However, I do know a couple of local antique dealers who have a reputation for underhand dealing. I may have a little nose around."

"Goodness, you are brave! Thank you, my dear."

Miss Miller smiled thinly.

Later that afternoon, she found herself standing outside Coombs, a rather down-at-heel antique shop of her acquaintance. Pride of place in the window display was claimed by a handsome Foreman piece. It certainly could have been one of Stella's, but it could just as easily have come from elsewhere.

She had barely taken five steps into the shop when Eli Coombs materialized. The owner of the shop, he was an oily man in his early sixties, given to cheap grey suits.

"What a delight to discover such a charming lady in my humble boutique," Coombs declared, making a sweeping bow. "How may I be of assistance?"

"I'm interested in the Foreman," Miss Miller told him.

"Oh, of course. What a wonderful eye you have. It's a lovely piece of work."

"I trust that you can verify its provenance."

"Of course, Madam. Every piece I stock is fully documented."

Miss Miller nodded. "I hope so. Given the recent Simmons burglary, one can't help but wonder."

"My dear lady, are you seriously trying to suggest …" Coombs' smile had vanished, and his accent had thickened quite noticeably too.

"Mr. Coombs, I am not your dear anything. Is that one of the stolen statuettes?"

"Preposterous!" Coombs spluttered. "I would never be party to such roguery. You could search everything I own from top to bottom and never find a hint of the other two. I can't remember ever being quite so insulted. Please leave at once."

"My apologies," Miss Miller said. "I meant no insult. I shall take my leave."

Exiting the shop, she went straight to the police station, and told the duty officer, "I can tell you who's fencing the goods stolen from the Simmons burglary."

How does she know that the statuette is definitely stolen?

HINT:
REPORTAGE.

 BLIND PANIC

Walter Mitchell had clearly dressed in a hurry. His trousers were belted but not buckled, his sweater was inside out and back to front, and his shoes were unlaced. His haste hadn't saved him, though. He had died at 8.23pm, shot through the heart on a quiet little street. The gun that killed him was found a few feet from his body, left there carelessly. The gunshot had been loud enough to attract attention, and a number of witnesses and potential suspects had been collected for Inspector Parnacki to interview.

The first witness, Maxim Davidson, was a butcher's assistant in his early twenties. He had been on his way home after a late day at work when he saw the victim. "He was running like he had the devil himself on his heels," Davidson said. "Which I suppose he must have done. He almost knocked me over as I turned onto the street. I stumbled back, and he just kept on going, not even a word of apology. When I heard the gunshot, I immediately thought of that silly sweater label vanishing into the distance. I saw a couple of other people in the area, a tall guy who looked kinda Irish, and a small, neat gentleman."

Patrick Carey worked as a builder, and had been at a bar in the area until shortly before the time of the murder. He was a tall, hard-bitten man in his thirties, powerful but starting to go to seed. "Sure and I heard a gunshot," he told Parnacki. "With a few pints under my belt, going to check seemed like a fine idea. Those same pints turned me around fiercely though, and I took my own sweet while to find my way to your victim. By the time I got there, your lad was already there, clucking over the body. There was a pistol across the way. Terrible. No, I didn't see anyone else while I was finding my way. Not so I noticed, anyway. I was distracted something powerful."

Braden Miles, a businessman, had been returning home from a friend's house. He was clearly still unsettled, and kept fiddling with his collar and tie. "I was a way up the street, but yes, I saw it happen. Merciful God. I'm not sure what drew my attention, but I looked back down the street and saw a person staggering to a halt in front of someone else. Then there was a sharp pop, and the

first person just collapsed. The second one immediately headed away back down the street, swiftly but without obvious haste, if you see what I mean. I just froze, I'm afraid. It was obvious what had happened, but I couldn't seem to focus enough to go to see if the victim had any chance. I just stood there. Next thing I knew, there were whistles, and your officer was talking to me. I wish I could tell you more, but honestly I couldn't even say for sure that they were both men, let alone any details."

Destiny Chavez worked as a waitress in a café on the street that Mitchell had been killed on. She was in her twenties, and had been cleaning tables at the time of the murder. "Yeah, I heard the shot. Little before that, I saw a guy hurrying past the window. He looked real dishevelled, that's why I noticed him. Couldn't be more than two minutes later when I heard it. I knew you boys would be round after that, so I stayed on after the cleaning was done. Sure enough, your officer turned up asking if I happened to have seen or heard anything. Well, that's what I saw, and what I heard. I can only hope it does you some good."

The interviews concluded, Parnacki permitted himself a satisfied smile. "Remind me to congratulate the officers on the scene," he told his assistant. "We've got the killer here already."

Who does Parnacki suspect and why?

HINT:
CLOTHING.

THE WATCHMAKER

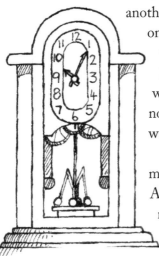

J. L. Jennings Watchmakers had been a fixture of the city for well over ten years. The aging Mr. Jennings was a stickler for precision and routine, as could reasonably be expected from a man who worked with timepieces. Miss Miller usually passed his shop at five to eleven in the morning, on her way to the weekly lunch meeting of the ornithological society. When she did, he was invariably sitting at his desk by the window, hunched over a mechanism of one sort or another. Very occasionally, he would be working on a casing. She always looked in and on those occasions when Jennings noticed her, they would exchange nods. So she was surprised and somewhat concerned to note, on that particular morning, that he was not in his usual place.

Deciding she could spare a couple of minutes, Miss Miller went into the shop. A bell jangled loudly above her. "Just a moment," came a voice from behind the curtain at the back. Less than a minute later, a young man in his thirties came out, straightening his jacket.

"You're not Mr. Jennings," Miss Miller said.

"No," said the man. "Well, that is, in fact yes, I am, but not the one you know. Eli Jennings. Pleased to meet you."

"Mary Miller," said Miss Miller. "Likewise. Is Mr. Jennings well?"

"Oh yes," Eli said. "Uncle Nick is fine. Strong as a horse. I'm sitting in for him this morning. He's off buying some faces for a set of carriage clocks."

"I see," Miss Miller said. "Do you help him like this often?"

"From time to time, but it's no bother. I'm very glad to be able to help. What else are family for?"

"What indeed."

"Did you need to speak to him personally?"

"Oh, no, thank you. I was just concerned as to his wellbeing. He's a familiar face, if you know what I mean."

Eli smiled. "Indeed I do. Well, while you're here, Uncle Nick does actually have something rather special in stock at the moment. A vintage table clock with the most exquisite mother-of-pearl fronting. A lady of your obvious refinement would find it rather enchanting, I think."

Miss Miller felt her eyebrow arching, and fought it back under control. "Well, I suppose that I can have a look at least."

Eli directed her attention to a table at the far end of the counter. Several pieces stood on it, including the clock in question. It was a genuinely lovely piece. The elegant fronting

was quite something to behold,
glimmering attractively. The
hands looked to be made
of gold but edged with jet
or basalt, so that they were
clearly delineated against both
the face and the hour markers.
The rest of the case was a mix of
gold and clear crystal, giving a
tantalizing glimpse into the
mechanisms inside.

"It certainly is
handsome," she told
him. "However, I'm not
sure that I—"

He named a price
which must have been
fifty percent of the
clock's value at the very
most. "You'd be doing
Uncle Nick a good turn," he
said. "The liquidity would be really
useful this morning."

"I'm afraid I can't," Miss Miller replied. "I must get to my
meeting."

"Of course," Eli said, looking disappointed. "It was a pleasure.

I'll pass on your concerns when Uncle Nick gets back."

"Thank you," she replied.

As soon as she got out of the shop, Miss Miller looked up and down the street. Spotting a police officer heading away, she hurried over, calling to him as she got close.

"Officer. Officer! I fear that something is terribly wrong at Jennings Watchmakers. Please, you must hurry!"

Why is Miss Miller concerned?

HINT:
NEPHEW.

THE SKYLARK

There are really only two ways to go in life if your parents christen you Skylark, and Skylark Cole had taken the name to heart. As free and flamboyant as the image suggested, she had been a source of delighted scandal and gossip ever since she had made her name. Now she was dead, stabbed through the heart in the dressing room of Peppersmiths, the lounge bar where she had sung.

"Did you ever meet her, Olly?" Melanie Rucker had worked at Peppersmiths for several years, helping performers with costume and make-up.

Oliver James shook his head. "Not in person. I saw her here a couple of times, though. She had a lovely voice."

"She was a lovely person. Totally carefree, but never mean with it."

"So I heard."

"It's a lot less common than you'd think, if you didn't work here. Most of the performers are quite difficult—not nasty people, but so easily made anxious by the tiniest thing, and always paranoid that they're losing their talent, or their looks. Either that, or they are terribly conceited, convinced that they're the next best thing to God. It must be a horrible way to live,

always on the absolute edge, with such massive ups and downs. Then there are a few who are just bitter and spiteful, and all you can do is keep out of their way. But Skylark was different. Totally innocent, in a lot of ways. She genuinely didn't seem to worry. Whatever came, she smiled and accepted it. Well, until …"

"I'm sorry, Mel," Oliver said.

"Thanks. Don't worry about me, though. I wasn't any closer to her than a couple of hundred other people were. It's just such a waste."

"Do the police have any leads?"

"They're thinking it was an obsessed fan or spurned lover. They searched the entire building as soon as they got here, but there weren't any intruders. As far as they can tell, someone surprised her in her room, then exited by the stage door. It wouldn't have been hard to escape."

"No?"

"Why don't you have a look at the route? You're so observant. You might find something they missed."

Oliver shrugged. "It seems unlikely, but I suppose you never know."

"Come on, let's look." Melanie dragged him out of Peppersmiths and round the side to the stage entrance. The alley was poorly lit, and would have been easy enough to sneak out of at either end. She pushed the side door open and ushered him into the backstage area, closing the door behind her. A serious, grey-haired woman was on a stool near the door.

"Julianne," Melanie said, "this is my pal Oliver. I can vouch for him."

Julianne nodded, and went back to the book she was reading.

Melanie bent close to Oliver's ear. "Management has someone here inside the door all the time now," she whispered. "It's the only way in. The murder weapon was found here." She scuffed a line with her toe just a couple of

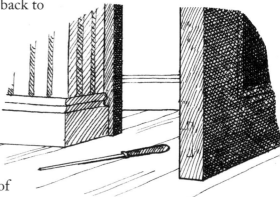

inches inside the door. The line was almost a foot long. "It was an eight-inch blade, pearl handle. Horrible." She grabbed his hand and tugged him along.

There were several doors leading off the corridor and a staircase leading up to the large dress closet, but no windows into any of the rooms. If no one were on the stairs or in the corridor at the time, and the doors were closed, it would be perfectly simple to both enter and escape the area unseen.

Melanie stopped in front of a door, one of several with a small silver star painted on it. "She was in here." She knocked on the door quickly, then poked her head in. "It's empty, come on."

Inside, the dressing room seemed innocuous enough. There was a well-lit mirror in front of a worktop which held a vase of flowers and a number of cosmetics and brushes. A chair sat underneath it. A couple of metal clothes racks took up most of the rest of the space. The floor was bare concrete.

"We had to take out the carpet," Melanie said, a little quaver in her voice. "You know."

Oliver nodded. "We need to talk to the police, Mel. The killer didn't escape down the corridor. I'm afraid that it was an inside job."

How does he know?

HINT:
KNIFE.

AN UNEXPECTED DEATH

Everyone was shocked when David Spencer died by suicide, but none more so than his sister, Claire.

"I don't understand it, Mary." Claire was holding herself together, but only by a fingernail.

Miss Miller squeezed Claire's hand. "It seems very odd," she said.

"It is odd," Claire said. "Very odd. Business was good, things were finally going well with Sheila, and Tom had just landed a decent job."

"Tom is the eldest son?"

Claire nodded. "Piers, the younger, is still at college."

"And you said he was getting on with Sheila again. How tough had it been?"

"They've been married for twenty-six years," she said, "but the last ten or so have been very hard. Some months they barely spoke. I tried not to pry, of course, but it was so nice to see them back to their old selves."

"Tragic," Miss Miller said.

Claire sighed, shakily. "I can't believe he's actually gone. Poor Sheila is utterly distraught."

"Forgive me asking," said Miss Miller. "What actually happened yesterday?"

"David was fine at breakfast, apart from a cough, but something in the post unsettled him. He refused to talk about it, but he became quite irritable, and spent most of the day in his office. It gave Sheila such a headache that by six o'clock, she'd taken to bed. I went out a little later. The museum had an evening exhibition of local seventeenth-century artworks, and Mia Perry and I went to see it. When I got back, I went to David's office to see if his temper had improved. He was …" She stifled a sob.

Miss Miller hugged her gently.

"Poor David was slumped sideways in his chair, his mouth open. He was so obviously dead. He'd pushed all his papers off the desk onto the floor. There was a bottle of pills in front of him."

"You called the police?"

"Immediately. They couldn't find any signs of a break-in, so they're happy it was suicide."

"I realize that this may seem like a difficult request, but may I see the room?" asked Miss Miller.

Claire frowned at her for a moment. "If you really want to, Mary."

David Spencer's office was thickly carpeted in green, with

plenty of lighting, and a window which looked out onto the garden. The main focus of the room was a large, leather-surfaced work desk and a sturdy, matching wing-backed chair. A mess of papers, folders, notes and newspapers was scattered on the floor to the left side of the desk. On top of it stood a single large pill-bottle, with several big pills beside it. Assorted paintings adorned the walls, and there were several bookshelves, crammed to overflowing with books and papers.

Claire shuddered. "I believe that the pills are meant to aid sleeping." Tears welled up in her eyes. "The police doctor said that he must have taken a score or more."

"Is this how the room was left?"

"Yes. I've kept it locked. It's too …" She trailed off.

"I'm so sorry, my dear," said Miss Miller. "I'm afraid your brother was murdered."

How does Miss Miller know?

HINT:
OFFICE.

FRIDAY NIGHT SPECIAL

Kal Knox died on Friday night. Several witnesses in the area heard the gunshot, placing the time of death at shortly after ten o'clock. Inspector Parnacki wasn't particularly surprised by the news. A low-rent career criminal, Knox had been violent, and although he had managed to avoid any murder convictions, he had never been likely to enjoy a long life. Appearances suggested that Knox had been going to a meeting of some sort. There was a note in his breast pocket, and although the bullet had ripped through it and blood had turned it into a soggy mess, the time 10:15 could still be made out.

The bullet that had been pulled out of him was a .38, and it matched the revolver the police had found in an industrial trash container a block away. It had been wiped down, but the lab was going over it to see if anything useful came up. In the meantime, three likely candidates had been brought in for questioning, and were waiting for Parnacki in separate interview rooms.

Lorenzo Holbrook was a local restaurateur with unproven ties to the mob. He was in his fifties and medium height with a stocky build. Bushy grey hair did nothing to disguise his calculating eyes.

Parnacki introduced himself and slapped a photo of the victim in front of Holbrook. "Do you know this man?"

Holbrook nodded. "Yeah. Knox, ain't it? He comes in the Olive Grove sometimes. Lousy tipper."

"Can you think of anyone who might wish Mr. Knox harm?"

"Nah. Can't say I know anyone who wishes him well either, mind."

"He was murdered last night."

Holbrook shrugged. "Is that so? Tragic. Tragic."

"What were you doing around 10pm last night?"

"Washing dishes," said Holbrook. "What else? I got three staff will vouch for it. I saw someone run down the alley behind my place, though. Little ferrety guy in a hat. It was dark. That's the best I can do, Inspector."

Toby Black was a cab driver who had done a stint in prison for armed robbery years before. "I was waiting for a fare who never showed," he explained. "Dispatch will tell you that. I saw your guy, must've been. He hung around for a bit, then checked the time and walked into an alley. It was just across the road from me. A moment later, a tall man in a heavy coat walked in behind him. I remember, because the newcomer was as bald as an egg. There was a pop, and your vic just collapsed. Poor guy never even got the chance to turn round. Then the bald man sprinted off past him, down the alley. I was going to go and see if I could help, really I was, but I was scared in case the bald guy decided to come back to doublecheck. If

there's one thing driving a cab has taught me, it's that you don't go looking for trouble. Not in this town."

The final interviewee, Jesse Hamby, worked in a local bar. Tall and muscular with short hair, he didn't bother hiding his resentment at being called in. When Parnacki showed him the photo, he shook his head silently.

"Are you sure?" asked Parnacki.

"Sure? Hell, no," Hamby sneered. "I see four hundred different guys in the bar every week."

"What were you doing around 10pm last night?"

"Walking home."

"Did you see or hear anything unusual?"

"You mean apart from a chunky old guy who almost smacked into me, and what looked like a dead man huddled in an alley? Nope."

Parnacki sighed. "What can you tell me about the dead man?"

Hamby tapped the photo. "You got his picture already."

"Thank you, Mr. Hamby. I'll be back shortly." Inspector Parnacki rose and left the room.

Outside, he turned to the officer guarding the interview rooms. "Make sure no one leaves. I have an arrest warrant to finalize."

Who is the murderer, and how does Parnacki know?

HINT:
WOUND.

 THE BREAK-IN

"**I** don't know what to tell you, Mr. James." Arlen Meier had worked for Oliver's father for three years, helping to look after the company's storage facility. "I feel terrible about it."

The thief had broken a board in the thin wooden ceiling to gain access to one of the rooms and had made off with a large amount of ornamental silverwork. Oliver sighed. "Why don't you talk me through it, Arlen?"

"I was doing my rounds when I heard something rattle in the metals room. I went in to have a look, and there was a pair of feet vanishing through a hole in the ceiling. I could see he'd been into the silver. I scrambled up there as best I could, but I couldn't see anything. By the time I got outside, he was long gone. I would have tried getting up into the rafters myself, but I'm not really built for that sort of thing."

Oliver nodded. It was difficult to imagine Arlen Meier even squeezing through a window, let alone a hole in the ceiling. "How did he know there was silver there? Wasn't it wrapped?"

Meier nodded mournfully. "Of course, Mr. James. All snug in that blue sheeting your father likes. Either he knew what he was looking for, or he just got lucky. He opened a few pallets before

he found the silver. But the delivery boys know the layout here well, and whoever delivered the silver would have been able to pinpoint the precise room without any trouble whatsoever."

"You didn't hear anything before then?"

"I'm really sorry, no, I didn't. I was out front, having a mug of tea. No one's been around all day. There's always traffic noise. He must have timed cutting through the wood to something loud going past. It's lucky I even got a glimpse of him."

"I suppose so," Oliver said. "We certainly don't blame you for not being everywhere at once. I should look at the metals room."

"Of course."

Meier escorted Oliver to the despoiled room. It was a horrible mess. At least a dozen blue tarpaulins had been slashed open, and bits of tarpaulin and thick string had been scattered everywhere. A tall stack of boxes had been pulled to the middle of the room, under a jagged hole in the ceiling. Chunks of wood and sawdust littered the room, covering everything. Several of the pallets of metals had been disturbed, but only the silver appeared to have been stolen.

"He must have been a strong lad, to make off with this much silver," Oliver said.

"I guess so," said Arlen. "He might have made several trips, for all I know."

"Yes, I suppose that's true." Brushing off the carpet of dust and splinters, Oliver pulled himself up the stack of boxes, and stuck his head into the hole. There was nothing interesting to see, just the dim, cavernous area between the ceiling and the slanted roof.

He jumped back down to the floor, and brushed himself off. "Okay, Arlen. Let's go through it again, and this time, how about telling me the truth?"

Why does Oliver think Arlen is lying?

HINT:
FLOOR.

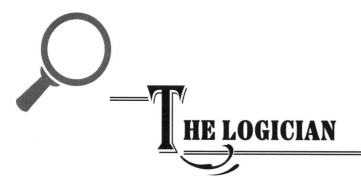

THE LOGICIAN

Inspector Parnacki was enjoying his Sunday morning newspaper when the call came. An hour later, he was standing outside the door of one Harold Rivera, a mathematician who worked for a large firm in the city. The detective on the scene opened the door to let him in.

"Good to have you here, Inspector," said the man. "My name's Burrell. I've spoken to the victim's cleaner and made a few enquiries, but it's not getting me anywhere."

"What can you tell me about the victim, Detective Burrell?"

"Harold Rivera, 48, lived alone. No spouse, children, or near family. Mathematician for Longmuir & Sons, accountants. He seems to have devoted his spare time to chess.

He had several regular chess partners, and very little social life otherwise. The body was found in the living room. He was killed by a blow to the head, twelve to twenty-four hours ago."

"I should have a look," said Parnacki.

"Of course." Burrell led him down the hall and into a modest living room.

There was a small couch and coffee table, but the room was dominated by a table holding a large, fine china chessboard. Two smaller tables, each with their own chessboard, were off to the side. Games were in progress on all three tables, but white appeared to be in a particularly strong position on the large table, with the middle of the board dominated by three adjacent mid-level pieces, the two white bishops separated by a white knight. The floor in front of the board was heavily stained with blood, as was the plain wooden chair lying on it.

"He lived alone?" asked Parnacki.

"Yes. A cleaner comes for two hours every day, generally mornings. She's the one who found him. Apparently the small tables were always mid-game,

and she was under extremely strict instruction never to touch them. He used them to keep track of play-by-mail games, he had told her. The big one was for face-to-face contests."

"I see," Parnacki said. "Do we have any idea of why anyone would want to kill a chess fanatic?"

"From what the cleaner said, he could be very rude at times. Accidentally, that is. No malice, just poor social skills. Way I see it, one of his chess pals finally snapped and killed him."

"Well, it might explain the game."

Burrell nodded. "We found a note on the coffee table. Three names. The cleaner confirmed it was the victim's handwriting, and said he often made notes of who to expect that day. To prepare himself, she said. Alphabetical order, sadly."

"Of course," said Parnacki. "How else would a logician order names?"

"Two are regular chess partners," Burrell said. "The third, it turns out he's a work colleague. Thomas Creech is a loner, like Rivera. Thirty-eight. A lawyer's assistant. I spoke to him—he said he was going to come over in the afternoon, but he had a cold, so he cried off. Matthew Norton is a bid-writer, forty-two. He's the other chess guy. He said he was going to visit in the evening, but he got distracted reading about bears, forgot the time and decided it was too late to visit. The colleague is Brendon Cotton. They work in the same section. He said he did come over, after lunch, to discuss a troublesome client account. It was something he did occasionally. He remembers noticing that the big chessboard was empty."

"Excellent work, Detective," Parnacki said. "You've solved the murder."

"I have?" Burrell sounded highly doubtful. "I thought I'd barely begun digging."

Parnacki nodded. "I can tell you who the murderer is right now."

Who killed Rivera, and how does Parnacki know?

HINT:
CHESSBOARD.

THE STOLEN STATUETTE

Anthony Long looked decidedly out of sorts. He was unusually pale, with dark smudges under his eyes, and his customary brisk gait had given way to a sullen slouch. Watching him approach, Oliver quickly decided to change plans and suggest a coffee shop, rather than the game he had obtained tickets for.

"You look dreadful," Oliver said, by way of greeting.

Anthony nodded. "Two hours sleep. Maybe less."

"Coffee?"

"You're a life-saver."

Ten minutes later, the men were seated at a quiet table in the corner of a café. As soon as the waitress was out of earshot, Anthony leaned forward. "I'm in a bit of a bind," he said, quietly. "I could do with some advice, Olly."

"You know I'll give it my best shot."

"Thanks. I had a break-in at the house yesterday."

"I'm sorry to hear that," Oliver said. "Did they take anything of value?"

Anthony nodded glumly. "Well, yes. The thief broke a window in the dining room and made off with a rather precious gold statuette from the hall. But that's not the problem. I was attending a meeting in town yesterday. Mrs. Chambers, my housekeeper, had the afternoon off. My brother Bill— he's been staying for a few days— was there, but he says he didn't hear anything."

Oliver arched an eyebrow at Anthony's curious phrasing. "He says?"

"He's even wilder than ever, Olly. I get the impression that he's only here because someone's trying to collect on a debt. I don't see why a thief would know to go straight for the statuette, ignoring some other nice pieces in the dining room. Bill suggested that the gardener's new lad might have seen something. Maybe he's right. But I can't help worrying that he might have taken it himself. If he has, the last thing I want to do is involve the police. Bill's a damn fool, but he is my brother. If it's not him, though, I'm risking repeat attacks, and I won't be able to claim for the loss."

"I understand completely," said Oliver, nodding. "Why don't

you show me the scene?"

A little while later, the men were round the back of the house. The broken window was a gaping mess. The flowerbed beneath showed signs of trampling. Oliver approached it carefully. There were several large footprints dug deep into the ground, with glass and shrubbery crushed into the soil in a pattern of sole that strongly suggested a work-boot of some kind. The prints were not visible on the grass of the lawn.

"Size ten, I'd say," said Oliver.

Anthony nodded. "Yes. Bill's a size seven, before you ask."

"Good, good. How about indoors?"

They went into the house, and Anthony led Oliver to the dining room. "The thief opened the window through the hole, then climbed in," Anthony said. "I've had the room left alone, in case the police need to see it. There's still a bit of mud on the sill of the broken window."

Oliver knelt down by the window and ran his hands over the carpet slowly. "There might be a little mud here, too." He straightened up, and put a sympathetic hand on Anthony's shoulder. "Let it drop, Tony. I'm afraid it was clearly your brother."

How does Oliver know?

HINT:
WINDOW.

THE INSIDE JOB

"Anthony Long tells me you helped him out of a tight spot, Oliver. Can I count on your discretion?" A slender man with glasses and prematurely thinning hair, Peter Smithson was a friend of Anthony's. Oliver had met him once or twice, and remembered him as pleasant enough.

"Of course," Oliver said.

"Thank you," said Peter, grabbing Oliver's hand and pumping it vigorously.

"Please don't mention it." Oliver gently disentangled himself. "How can I help?"

"Someone stole a lot of money, and the ledgers, from my office safe. Didn't touch anything else. I got lucky—we found the whole haul again. They'd stashed it outside, under a tarpaulin. Abby, from Wilson's downstairs, was working late and noticed a bundle being hidden. She became suspicious and went to look, and immediately realized what she'd found. I'd have been totally destroyed without her intervention. But the best she could do by way of a description was 'a tall man'."

"Sounds like a close escape," Oliver said.

"The thing is, only my clerks know how to get into the safe. It's got to be one of them, sadly. I'm hoping to resolve this quietly. Things are rocky enough at the moment without a scandal on top."

Oliver nodded. "I understand, and I'll try to help. Tell me about your clerks."

"There are three of them, Simon, Abel, and Emmett, all of a similar height. I know it's a rotten way to spend a Saturday, but perhaps you'd speak to them yourself? I've asked them to be at their homes."

So, ninety minutes later, Oliver found himself being introduced to Simon Thurston, a tall young man who had a room in an undistinguished boarding house.

"Thank you for seeing us," Peter began. "This is Oliver James, a friend of mine. There was a theft at the office yesterday evening, shortly after work. I wanted to know if you might have spotted anything unusual."

Simon hung his head. "I'm sorry, Mr. Smithson. I left a little early last night, because I wasn't feeling so good. Everything was fine when I left."

"Would the landlady vouch for your presence?" asked Oliver.

Simon blinked at him. "I ... Well, perhaps. She doesn't pay much attention to us."

"I see," Oliver said. "That's all, for now. Thank you for your time."

Abel Pena lived in a busy apartment block. He was older than Simon Thurston, and his apartment had seen better days. Peter repeated his introduction, and Abel peered at the two men thoughtfully.

"I left on time and locked up. There were plenty of people still working in other offices. There wasn't anyone hanging around outside the building, and I didn't see anything out of the ordinary. I walked home via the park and had a quiet evening."

Oliver nodded. "Did you notice if Wilson's office was still open when you left?"

"Yes, actually. I saw a few people at their desks through the window." Abel paused. "You suspect an inside job?"

Peter started a denial, but Oliver stopped him. "It's possible," he said.

Abel nodded. "Well, I should probably mention that Thurston sneaks off early any time you're not in the office yourself, Mr. Smithson. It seemed harmless enough, but given the circumstances ..."

Peter stiffened, and Oliver placed a hand on his arm.

"Thank you," Peter managed. "I appreciate your speaking frankly."

"We may have a few more questions," Oliver said. "Thanks

for your time."

Emmett Sterling lived in a pleasant little town house with his wife, Charlotte. Peter and Oliver joined the couple in their sitting room and Peter repeated his introduction once again.

Emmett thought for a moment. "I left slightly early to pick up some dry cleaning. I got back home at the usual time and was here all evening."

Charlotte nodded.

Emmett tapped his chin. "Have you spoken to Thurston? He's a sneaky little weasel, always creeping off, and he's desperately hard up. If any of us would rob your safe, he would."

"Do you know why he's so hard up?" asked Oliver.

"I reckon he gambles," Emmett said. "Probably desperate to repay a debt to some shady moneylender."

"I see," said Oliver. "What about Abel?"

"He's one of those quiet fish. I don't think he's the sort, though."

"Thank you," said Oliver. "We might have a few more questions later."

Once they were outside, Oliver turned to Peter. "Sure you don't want to call the police? I know who your thief is."

Who is the thief, and how does Oliver know?

HINT:
SAFE.

A keen member of the Ornithological Society, Miss Miller was delighted by the chance to visit Mattingley Chase, whose extensive grounds included an area of marshland that attracted rare species. The owner, Kyler Mattingley, was a noted recluse, but ornithology was his passion, so he had agreed to allow four Society members to stay for the weekend.

The guests were familiar to each other from exchanges in the Society's journal, *Tweetings*. The ride to the Chase was the first time they had actually met, however.

They were a merry bunch. Miss Wilson was the youngest of the quartet, fashionably dressed, with a special interest in finches and an enthusiasm for photography. Austin Ball was charming and magnificently attired in a cream jacket, dark trousers, black boots and silk kerchief. Clayton Hendricks was an outdoor type, strongly built, with a large beard.

Their conversation was dominated by thoughts of Kyler Mattingley.

"I hear tell that Mr. Mattingley is an impeccably gracious host," said Miss Miller.

"A cautious one," Hendricks replied.

Miss Wilson smiled.

"We're very lucky," she said.

"Indeed we are," said Hendricks.

"We shall just have to ensure that the great Mr. Mattingley has no reason to be displeased with our presence," Ball said. "Maybe that way we can hasten the day when this opportunity is extended to other members of the Society."

Miss Miller nodded. "Quite. I assume we all remembered our gifts?"

"Of course," said Hendricks. "I have brought him a book of doves; the illustrations are magnificent."

"That sounds delightful, Mr. Hendricks," said Miss Wilson. "I'll have to ask Mr. Mattingley for a look."

When they arrived at the Chase, they were met by Gustav, Mr. Mattingley's man, who showed them to their rooms.

Miss Miller's bedroom was charming. A comfortable bed and tasteful décor were complemented by a selection of beautiful artworks of birds. There were several sketches, a silver-backed mirror engraved with owls, a small, graceful carving of a jade heron in flight, and a wooden bookend in the form of a woodpecker. But what really caught her eye was a striking oil painting of birds of paradise.

After refreshing themselves, the guests assembled downstairs, clutching their gifts. Kyler Mattingley was there to greet them.

"Welcome, my friends," he said, smiling. "I so rarely meet people, but I feel as if I know you all already. Where would we be without your lovely studies, Miss Wilson, or, Mr. Ball, your hilarious anecdotes?"

After cocktails, the party went into the dining room, where they were served an impressive meal. Afterwards, he opened their gifts with every appearance of delight.

Miss Miller had brought a dozen hand-carved whistles in the likeness of less common woodland birds, in a lacquer box. When blown, each one made the trill of the bird it resembled. Hendricks presented Mattingley with the book of doves, each illustration a masterpiece of both art and biology. Ball gave a rather elegant jade phoenix, caught in the moment of its fiery rebirth, cleverly wrapped in silk. Miss Wilson, finally, had prepared a series of photographic exposures showing the changes in a park near her home over the course of a year, bound in red leather. Eventually they retired early, to facilitate a dawn start.

Miss Miller had barely dozed off when she was awoken by a heavy knock, and Gustav entered.

"Ah, you at least are in place. Forgive me for disturbing you, Madam, but Mr. Mattingley has been murdered. Your companions are not in their rooms."

"I shall come down directly," said Miss Miller.

By the time she was dressed and downstairs, the other Society members had been gathered.

"They say Kyler Mattingley is dead!" Miss Wilson exclaimed.

"So I hear," said Miss Miller. "It's a terrible business. I was in bed."

Miss Wilson paused. "I was in the dining room, actually. I wanted to look at Mr. Hendricks' book."

"I was in the drawing room, enjoying a cigar," said Ball. "It is my invariable habit."

Hendricks shrugged. "Well, I was in the kitchen. I need milk to take my medicine with."

Miss Miller waved to the manservant. "May I have a word, Mr. Gustav?" He nodded, and she crossed over to him. "I fear that I know who the killer is."

Who is the assassin, and how does Miss Miller know?

HINT:
GIFTS.

HE GEM SHOP

T he peeling sign above the gem shop read 'BALDWIN & SONS', and if the date were to be believed, it had been in business for more than thirty years. The window displays were orderly, if empty, but the open door was hanging at an odd angle. A bored-looking police officer stood in front of it. As Inspector Parnacki approached, the man pulled himself properly erect and saluted sharply.

"Sir, good morning," he said.

Parnacki nodded politely. "Has anyone been in or out of the shop?"

"Not since I've been here, sir."

"Good work."

The robbery was much more obvious once Parnacki entered the shop. Many of the cupboards showed signs of having been forced open and empty trays were strewn all over the floors and glass counters. If there was a single valuable jewel left in the place, it was well out of sight.

A tall, unhappy man stood in the middle of the chaos. He was well-dressed, but in some considerable disarray, and there was a nasty-looking bruise at the side of his forehead. Parnacki went straight to him.

"Mr. Henry Baldwin?" the inspector asked.

The man nodded.

"I am Inspector Parnacki."

Baldwin looked surprised. "Paddington Parnacki?"

"So the newspapers dub me," the inspector sighed.

"Sorry, Inspector. Your fame precedes you."

"No matter. Would you please tell me what happened, in your own words?"

Baldwin nodded. "I was closing up last night. Sometimes one of my assistants stays behind to help, but they were both keen to get off swiftly. Their names are Alec Cardue and Scott Benedict. I have their addresses."

"The events of last night first, please," said Parnacki.

"Sorry. I'm still a little rattled. I'd finished locking all the precious pieces away—" he gestured at the broken cupboards, "—and turning the lights off, and I was just opening the door to start barring the windows. As I did so, a dark figure in a tall hat crashed through the door, throwing me back. I staggered, and then he hit me hard on the head with a cosh of some sort.

I didn't get a good look at him. It was night already, you see. Anyhow, I fell over, and cracked the back of my head on the floor. Drove the wits from me. I was dimly aware of the noise of the cupboards being broken into. I didn't realize until later that he was also grabbing the trays and tipping the contents into his silk sack. It all seemed disconnected, somehow. I must have passed out at some point. When I came round, it was already light. I remembered the assault, discovered that I'd been totally cleaned out, and called the police. That was about an hour and a half ago."

Parnacki nodded. "You mentioned your assistants?"

"It feels like an inside job, you know? I had bought a new batch of stock three days ago, and anyway, you'd need to know my routine to judge exactly when to break in like that. It seems impossible to imagine either of them doing this, but they're both around the right build. Alec has a new girlfriend, too, and Scott likes his cards."

"Don't concern yourself, Mr. Baldwin. I already know the culprit."

"You do?"

Parnacki nodded gravely.

Who is the thief? How does Parnacki know?

HINT:
TESTIMONY.

VICTOR'S FUNERAL

Victor Ivanova had a rather successful funeral, all things considered. The service was appropriately moving, the burial went smoothly, and they even managed to find some people to say kind things about him. His evil temper and ready fists were glossed over as a "passionate nature". Apparently, getting shot earned one a certain measure of posthumous tolerance.

At the wake afterwards, Miss Miller availed herself of some tea and a small crustless sandwich and set out to circulate. Although the police had yet to rule on whether Victor had died by suicide or been murdered, his supposed mourners seemed to have very little collective doubt.

"Of course he was murdered!" At just 20, Kailee Williams was still rather excitable, and seemed to be enjoying herself thoroughly. Her beau, Eugene, was Victor's son. "It's wrong to speak ill of the dead, but poor dear Eugene suffered terribly for his father's moods. But so many others did too. Men like Victor don't die by suicide. They don't have the self-awareness. They just hang around forever, getting older and meaner and older and meaner. I bet it was the gardener. Victor actually whipped him, once. Can you imagine? Whipping a gardener? It chills the blood, I tell you."

Chance Hoffs was a long-standing friend of the family. "Victor always was a difficult man," he said. "He got worse as the years ticked by. I don't think I'll ever really know what was sticking in his craw, but the frustration and anger seemed to grow. He made it to his forties, which honestly is about as far as most people ever expected. I don't suppose we'll ever really know the truth of it. The nearest thing to a witness was his great-aunt in the next room, but she's as deaf as a stump, and didn't hear a thing."

Eventually, Miss Miller tracked down Victor's great-aunt, Agatha, to a sunny corner of the room. She was a spry-looking octogenarian with bright, lively eyes and a large ear trumpet.

"Hello. I'm Mary Miller," said Miss Miller, joining Agatha at her table.

The old lady held up a forbidding finger, then laboriously swung the ear trumpet into place, jamming one end into her ear, and pointing the other directly at Miss Miller's mouth. "What was that, my dear?" Her voice was surprisingly steady.

"I said hello, and that my name is Mary Miller."

"Agatha Ivanova. Delighted to meet you. Did you know my great-nephew?"

"Socially," said Miss Miller.

"Ah, by far the best way. Poor man. There were devils inside him, you know." She paused. "Metaphorical devils, that is, not literal ones. I haven't lost my mind just yet. Victor could be quite charming when everything was going his way. He never could bear to be thwarted. But then his father, my nephew, was quite the tyrant in his time. It's so silly, this violence and scorn that men heap on their sons."

"Eugene seems quite nice," Miss Miller said.

"Yes, indeed. He was shielded by his mother—literally, often. Victor's violence was relatively easy to deflect, if one were prepared to pay the cost. There is marble in that woman's spine, I tell you."

Recalling Briony Ivanova's firm, composed appearance at the funeral, Miss Miller could only agree. The widow was towards the middle of the room at the moment, talking with several guests. A bellow of anger erupted from the far side of the room. Agatha and Miss Miller looked round together. A weathered-looking man was being calmed by several other people.

"Victor's gardener," Agatha said. "He has a lot to be angry about."

"Do you think he might be the killer?"

Agatha's eyebrows raised at that, and she chuckled. "Well, I suppose he might be. No use asking me, my dear."

"You were in the next room," said Miss Miller.

"Quite so, but I'm afraid I was reading. If anyone walked past my door, I didn't see them."

"So you didn't hear any arguments?"

"I didn't even hear the gunshot," Agatha said. "I wouldn't hear the last trump itself unless I was pointing this beast straight at it." She patted her ear trumpet with her free hand.

"No, of course," Miss Miller said. "But you must have some suspicions."

Agatha nodded. "Honestly, I suspect he died by his own hand. I like to imagine that he had a moment of lucidity, and realized that the only way to stop himself from destroying his son was to end his own life. One concluding moment of actually being a father." She sighed. "I'm glad that Eugene has that nice Miss Williams to help him through this. She reminds me a little of his mother—kind and bright, with a core of steel. I'm quite sure you know the type, my dear." She shot Miss Miller a very knowing look.

Miss Miller smiled politely. Oh dear, she thought. Who are you covering up for, Agatha?

How does Miss Miller know that the old lady is lying?

HINT:
GARDENER

THE CARYATIDS

Taking a deep breath, Oliver James knocked on his father's office door and went in.

"Ah, there you are, m'boy." At 6ft, Cameron James was just a little shorter than his son, but where Oliver was trim, his father had the broad power of a man who'd spent most of his life handling large amounts of stone and brick. "Come in, come in. Jacob and I were just discussing ornamentation for the Southwell building. Thought maybe you could lend a hand."

Oliver winced, and braced himself. Cameron still hadn't come to terms with his son's preference for architectural design over actual construction, and the lectures about his future were getting tediously frequent.

"Do you remember Pick & Sons, Oliver?" Now in his forties, Jacob York had been his father's right-hand man for as long as Oliver could remember. He at least was on Oliver's side regarding architecture.

Oliver nodded.

"Cruz has a line on a couple of Roman statues at a very good price," Cameron said.

"Maybe too good," Jacob added.

"Maybe, maybe," said Cameron. "But if not, they'd fulfil Southwell's requirements for the frontispiece and then some, considerably under budget as well. You've got a good eye, Oliver. I thought maybe you'd give us your opinion on the matter."

A relieved Oliver said he'd be delighted to help.

"Pull up a seat," Cameron said, waving at the pile of paperwork on his desk.

Oliver sat down and ran his eye over the details. According to the papers, the statues were a matched pair of elegant caryatid columns from the reign of the Roman emperor Diocletian, in surprisingly good condition. The date of construction was clear, since the sculptor had marked the bases with his own name, Emperor Diocletian's full titles, and the year, AD 302. That year marked the start of the emperor's bloody persecution of the Christians, during which every Roman citizen was compelled to offer sacrifices to the Greek gods. Some venues had undoubtedly been constructed for the purpose, and caryatids—supporting columns in the form of a woman—while not common in Roman times, were not unheard of either.

From the pictures that had been included, the statues looked as if they were made from marble. There was some wear and tear—it would have been miraculous if there hadn't been—but even so, the pieces could quite easily have been in a museum.

Oliver looked up. "Where did Pick find them?"

"He got them from a Turkish fellow," Cameron said. "The man said that they'd been sold to him by an Ottoman pasha who'd fallen on hard times, having had them in his family since the time of the Seljuks in the 13th century."

"There is some supporting documentation," Jacob said.

"Well, it's not totally impossible for a couple of Diocletian pieces to have survived in private collections," Oliver said. "Diocletian was in Antioch for several years, up to AD 302 at least. I can see temples being raised in his name, and then statuary being purloined later, as the empire shrank. In this case, however, I feel comfortable saying that these pieces are absolutely and definitely fakes. Sorry, father."

How can Oliver be so sure?

HINT:
DIONYSIAN.

DEADLY RENDEZVOUS

The murder of Angela Voss—in the middle of Tate's Wine Bar no less—set all the gossip sheets buzzing. When the papers learned that "Paddington" Parnacki was leading the investigation, the story became front-page news.

The facts, such as they were, seemed broadly unpromising at first glance. Mrs. Voss had met a pair of friends at the venue, Elizabeth Hansen and Sophia Rosenthal. Voss and Hansen had shared a pitcher of a light wine cocktail, while Rosenthal had opted for a coffee. The ladies had consumed nothing else. Ninety minutes later, Voss was dead, apparently poisoned.

While everything was being tested, Inspector Parnacki conducted interviews, starting with the waiter who had served the three women.

Michael Johnson was a tall, pleasant-seeming man in his late twenties. He was clearly nervous, and kept rubbing the palms of his hands on the sides of his shirt.

"You waited on Mrs. Voss and her friends, I believe," Parnacki began.

"Yes, sir," Johnson said. He paused, then blurted out, "Am I going to prison?"

Parnacki raised an eyebrow. "Are you telling me that you murdered Mrs. Voss?"

"No! Uh, that is, no, sir. Not on purpose. But I served their drinks, didn't I? So … so I killed her."

Parnacki attempted to calm him. "Even if that's true, merely serving the drink would make you no more responsible than the tray you were carrying. Unless, of course, you knew the drink was poisoned."

Johnson sagged with relief. "Oh, thank heaven." He wiped the corners of his eyes. "So, how can I help?"

Parnacki smiled encouragingly. "You are familiar with the three ladies, I take it?"

"Yes. They're regular customers. Were regular customers, I suppose."

"Tell me what happened."

"Well, I took the ladies' coats and scarves, and seated them at their usual table, by the fire. Mrs. Rosenthal ordered a coffee with cream, and Mrs. Hansen asked for a jug of the iced wine cup to share with Mrs. Voss. I took the order to the bar, and went to attend to some other regulars, the Timothys, who'd indicated that they wanted me. By the time I'd taken their order, the ladies' drinks were ready. I took them over to their table, along with a pair of wine glasses. I set the drinks on the table, poured for Mrs. Voss and Mrs. Hansen, then I left them to it. Mrs. Hansen seemed thirsty. Mrs. Rosenthal asked for a little honey, which I fetched. That was it, until …"

"Until?"

Johnson swallowed nervously. "It was a bit over an hour. Mrs. Voss got to her feet in some distress. She called for cold water. Before I could fetch it, she'd gone into a coughing fit. Then she fell over and went into convulsions, and died shortly afterwards. Her friends were distraught."

"Was it usual for Mrs. Rosenthal to order coffee?"

"Quite usual, yes. She never drinks any alcohol, at least not that I have ever seen."

"I see. And did the barman start with Tate's

within the last month?"

"Why yes, actually. This is his second week. Do you want me to fetch him? I'm sure he's here."

"Not just yet, Mr. Johnson. I may have some further questions soon."

As Inspector Parnacki left the troubled waiter, an officer approached. "Reports, sir," the man said. "Just in." Parnacki took the papers with a nod of thanks, and glanced through them. The contents of the table were listed as one pitcher, quarter-full; one glass, half-full; one glass, full; one coffee pot, empty; one cream salver, empty; one honey dish, two-thirds full; and one coffee cup, empty. The pitcher and both glasses were laden with arsenic.

Nodding to himself, Parnacki looked up at the officer. "We need to focus our attention on Elizabeth Hansen," he said. "Have her brought in for questioning."

Why does Parnacki suspect Hansen?

HINT:
THIRST.

THE BODY IN THE STUDY

When Colonel Herbert was found dead in his study one morning with a knife through his neck, suspicion fell on the members of his household. There were no signs of forced entry anywhere in the building, and no public impropriety on the Colonel's part to make enemies. As police scrutiny intensified, the Colonel's sister Vivienne consulted her friend, Mary Miller, who had an almost obsessive interest in mystery stories and made a hobby of deduction.

"The thing is, my dear," Vivienne said, "the police are quite right to be looking at the household. William was a pillar of the community, but in private he was positively beastly. We were all terrified of him, and he would fly into the most violent rage over the tiniest thing. He saw off every suitor I ever had, even one or two I was quite fond of. If the culprit isn't found, I fear that I might end up spending my twilight years in prison."

It was therefore agreed that Miss Miller should talk to the entire household, one at a time, about the fatal evening.

"We'll have to start with you, Vivienne," Mary said.

"Me?" Vivienne looked shocked.

"Who else?"

"Of course," she sighed.

"Wonderful. Please do have a seat. Tea? No? Very well. So, what transpired?"

"Well, you know most of it. My brother was in his study on Monday night, taking care of some paperwork. I left him to it, and went to bed at around ten o'clock. Sophie, the maid, went into the study to tidy a little after seven the following morning. That's when she discovered the body. She shrieked persistently enough to wake the whole place up. The police said that he must have died before midnight."

Next came the maid, Sophie. "It was horrible, ma'am. The Colonel was still in his study when I went up before eleven. I could see the light under his door. Miss Herbert was already asleep, I could hear her, on account of my room being below hers. Next morning I got up at me usual time, five-thirty, did the fires, cleaned the kitchen floor, and started on me rounds. I opened the study door and there he was, dead as a fish. I slammed the door shut and screamed me head off. Couldn't bring meself to go into the room. Mr. Hunt was the first to get to me."

Hunt was the family butler. "I returned from seeing Cook home at nine forty-five that evening. Miss Herbert went to bed shortly afterwards, and the maid wasn't much later. I went to my bed after she'd retired. I looked in on the Colonel before doing

so, to ensure he had no further needs for the evening. I was breakfasting the following morning when I heard the screams. I discovered the maid in considerable distress outside the study. Cook arrived a moment behind me, so while she consoled the girl, I opened the door to investigate. I understood her distress as soon as I got the light on. Colonel Herbert was quite dead, having vented a lot of blood. The carpet is completely ruined, I'm sad to say."

The cook, Mrs. Palletier, seemed unbothered by events. "I don't like speaking ill of the dead, but womankind is safer without that man walking this earth, let me tell you. I heard Sophie's screams and made my way to the Colonel's study. Hunt flicked the lights on, and I heard him gasp a little. The old man was dead as a doorjamb. Personally, I reckon the gardener did him in."

The gardener, Lou Dotson, was curt about the whole affair. "I was home on Monday, with my wife. When I came in Tuesday, the old buzzard was already dead. I need to get back to the roses."

With everyone interviewed, Mary called Vivienne back in. She hugged her friend and said, "Good news. I know who killed him."

Who is the murderer, and what tipped Miss Miller off?

HINT:
LIGHT.

HE SUICIDE

J effrey Alston had always had a flair for the dramatic. Never happier than when he was the object of attention, he was prone to childish stunts such as setting fire to his moustache-tips or juggling with priceless vases. His one great terror was of loneliness, and he always suffered greatly when he was forced to spend time in his own company. So Miss Miller

was not completely surprised when she heard the news that he had died. She prepared a small basket of food and went round to the house to see if there was anything she could do for Natalie, his widow.

It turned out that Natalie was not coping well. She threw herself on Miss Miller and sobbed loudly for several minutes. Once she had composed herself, the story came out.

"I just don't

understand it, Mary. I don't even know for certain whether he meant to kill himself, or if it was one of his capers gone wrong."

Miss Miller frowned. "Kill himself?"

"Exactly! Jeff hadn't been himself for weeks—subdued, a bit snappy even—but I'd never have dreamed that he'd decide to take his own life. But really, it's difficult to see what else he could have been doing. I was visiting my mother on Sunday. While I was out, he sealed himself in his office. Literally, I mean. There was thick tape all around the doorframe, closing up all the cracks. The same on the window. Then he knifed open the gas line, and … and waited quietly to suffocate." She suppressed several loud sobs.

"I'm so sorry, Natalie. What a terrible thing."

"It's as if I'm stuck in some terrible nightmare laid on by a villain with an exceedingly dark sense of fun. I keep expecting to, oh, I don't know, have a gigantic toy bear waddle into the room roaring or something." She sank down even more. "It would be easier if I could think of it as some lunatic stunt he was trying to attempt. When I first saw his door taped up like that, that was my

first thought. I had to get Brock to cut the frame open. But then we went in, and … I don't remember much about the rest of the afternoon, mercifully. Brock called for the police. They seem happy enough with suicide. They discovered the gas line. But there's no note, so I just don't know. My brain won't rest from trying to find alternatives. But I can't come up with anything that's not flat-out ludicrous."

"I totally understand," said Miss Miller. "Hmm. Gas. Some sort of misguided attempt at inducing a type of mesmerism, perhaps?"

Natalie shook her head. "Jeff thoroughly disliked that sort of bunkum. He much preferred the real world."

"A science experiment?"

"That's much more his style, but there was nothing to experiment on. Except himself, I suppose. But I don't think he was quite that foolish."

"Pyrotechnics, perhaps. If he dozed off while trying to prepare some sort of specific gas level …" Miss Miller's voice trailed off as a nasty thought hit her. "Oh, Natalie. It wasn't a crazy misadventure. Jeffrey was murdered."

How does Miss Miller know?

HINT:
DOOR.

THE MISER

Walking briskly through the park, Inspector Parnacki took a long draw on his pipe and tried to clear his mind. Fact: Karson Meyers was dead and, apparently, almost completely unlamented. Fact: Meyers had been stabbed through the throat with a poker snatched from beside the fire in his sitting room. Fact: Time of death looked to be somewhere between 7pm and 11pm. Fact: The maid had caught sight of Meyers lying on the floor in a pool of blood shortly before breakfast and raised the alarm. Fact: She had told a number of curious enquirers that the murder weapon had been a poker before he'd had a chance to ask her to stop, unfortunately. Fact: Half a dozen people had motive to want the old miser dead, the opportunity to have done it, and a reasonable if flimsy alibi. Fact: Having interviewed all six, he didn't seem to be any closer to identifying a suspect.

Such a state of affairs irked the proud Parnacki. Puffing on his pipe, he thought back on the various interviews.

Michael Knight was a lumber distributor, and one of Meyers' most vocal creditors. The two had been doing business for several years, but Meyers now owed him a substantial sum of money. According to Knight, Meyers had steadfastly refused to settle the debt. "I'm not surprised someone did him in," Knight had said. "He was infuriating. It wasn't me, though. I was at home with my wife all evening. Besides, I don't hold out hope of getting any money out of his estate. Unfortunately, he owed me the money personally, rather than through his firm."

Susan Hugo was Meyers' long-estranged daughter, his only child. She was having a difficult time of it financially, and might possibly have hoped that she would be the main beneficiary of whatever her father had to leave. "I'd love to feel sad that he's dead," she had said. "One ought to feel sad when one's father dies. But the truth is that he was never pleasant to me or my mother. I haven't been alone in a room with him since Mother died, and that was fifteen years ago. But being murdered with a poker, that's horrible. I suppose I feel a bit sad about that. My husband, Paul, is sick at the moment. I was looking after him. I understand that you have to ask. He'll confirm my alibi."

Ian Goddard, one of Meyers' managers, was unusually forthright in his interview. "I'm absolutely delighted that the

old son of a bitch is dead. He was a coward, a bully and a skinflint, and he made my life miserable. Maybe now we'll have a chance of getting the firm back onto a firm footing. I thought about killing him myself, you know. Repeatedly. But he wasn't worth it. I was playing bridge last night, with three friends. I can even give you a run-down of how the hands played out, if you want."

Evan Patterson was the other manager. He seemed more reflective than bitter about the victim. "It's difficult to think of him as dead, let alone stabbed. He was such a dominating presence. He only had to walk into a room, and it seemed as though all the air vanished. We shouldn't speak ill of the dead, but God help me, I won't miss him. The company won't miss him, either. I suppose we'll have to put out some regretful-sounding statement and have an official day of mourning or something. I had dinner with my brother last night."

Emma Moss was Meyers' housekeeper. Her interview was short and to the point. "Heard he was dead." Pressed on her whereabouts for the evening in question, she grudgingly added "Home, of course, with my family."

Jerrold Stanton was Meyers' butler. "I never had an employer like Mr. Meyers. Oh, my. What a broken man. I tried to leave, six years ago, as soon as I realized exactly what sort he was. He made it clear that if I did, he'd accuse me of theft and bribe the judge to send me to prison. I never dared even hint of leaving again. It's been hard, but I kept my head down, and did as I was told. It's time for a new chapter in my life. I was at the bar last night, having a beer or two."

Parnacki suddenly stopped dead. "Stupid of me," he said. "Stupid!" He immediately turned on his heel, and hurried back towards the station.

Who is the killer, and how does Parnacki know?

HINT:
POKER.

THE NECKLACE

It was past 9pm when Inspector Parnacki arrived at the home of Jackson and Isabella Stone. The snow that had been falling all day had finally stopped a couple of hours earlier, so the journey hadn't been too unpleasant. He was met at the top of the driveway by a chilly-looking policeman. Parnacki showed the man his badge, and asked for a report.

The officer began, "An extremely valuable diamond necklace belonging to Isabella Stone was stolen from the house an hour ago, sir. Mr. and Mrs. Stone are entertaining longstanding friends this evening, a couple named John and  Kathleen Acosta. None of the four report noticing anything suspicious until Mr. Stone discovered that a ladder had been placed against the side wall, leading up to the window of the main bedroom. The group searched the house and he found that the necklace had been stolen. I have personally verified that the intruder is not anywhere to be found at the scene. He must have climbed in and out, and made his escape before anyone noticed. Everything was in order when the Acostas arrived at 5.30pm, but the crime could have taken place any time between then and 8.30pm, when the theft was discovered."

Parnacki thanked the officer and asked to be shown the ladder. He was then led round the front of the house to the side. The snow was a mess of footprints, both around the house and to and from the small garden shed. The ladder had been placed carefully against the side of the building, reaching up to an open window. Was that something flapping? Parnacki took hold of the ladder and squinted up at the window, flinching slightly as the ladder sank into the snow. The flapping turned out to be just a piece of curtain blowing around in the breeze.

"It came from the shed?"
The officer nodded.

"Jackson Stone positively identified it."

"I should have a word with the Stones and the Acostas," Parnacki said.

The two men then went inside the house and into the sitting room, where the four friends were gathered. It was a pleasant room, neatly furnished and tidy, comfortable rather than prosperous.

After the introductions, Parnacki asked the four to give him their accounts of what had happened.

"We didn't realize anything had happened," said Isabella Stone. "Not until it was all over, anyway."

"Yes," said Jackson Stone. "I went to the bathroom a little before 8.30, and spotted from the window that the ladder was resting against the wall. I couldn't make sense of it, so once I was finished I popped outside to check, and there it was, out of the shed and running straight up to the bedroom window. So I came back inside and raised the alarm."

John Acosta nodded in agreement. "Jack rushed into the room looking most alarmed, and told us there might be an intruder in the house. He and I immediately checked to make sure we were safe, while the ladies telephoned the police. I searched downstairs, while Jack looked upstairs. I was quite relieved to discover that no knives appeared to be missing from the kitchen."

"That's when I discovered that Isabella's necklace was missing, and the thief with it," Jackson said.

"We checked everywhere, inside and out," said Kathleen Acosta. "No sign of either the necklace or the thief. It's quite alarming."

Inspector Parnacki nodded thoughtfully. "And I suppose the four of you have been together all evening?"

"Of course," said Isabella. "In pairs, anyway. Kathy and I have made a couple of trips to the kitchen."

"I see," Parnacki said. "I should remind you, Mr. Stone, that insurance fraud can carry a very significant prison sentence. I trust that the necklace will be found dropped in some suitably convenient location."

Stone paled, and the other three gasped.

"Good evening," Parnacki said, and sauntered out.

Why does Parnacki think Jackson Stone is the thief?

HINT:
LADDER.

THE SAILOR

Oliver James' father, Cameron, clapped him warmly on the shoulder. "Oliver, good to see you. I'd like you to meet Frank Cuevas. He's the captain of the schooner *Emma*, out of Dunedin. Damien Walters introduced us at my club yesterday evening. Frank, this is Oliver, my eldest. He'll take over the reins from me sooner or later, come what may."

Suppressing a groan at the thought of a career as a builder, Oliver smiled and said, "It's a pleasure, Captain Cuevas."

"Just Frank, please," said the captain.

"We've been talking about ebony, Oliver," Cameron said.

"Ah," said Oliver.

"There's always a lot of demand for ebony finishings, Frank. I can probably make good use of whatever you can lay your hands on."

Cuevas smiled. "That's good to hear. The Dutch East Indies are groaning with the stuff. Did you know that the archipelago has more than 15,000 different islands, and more than 50,000 miles of coastline with it? Most of them are tiny little flyspecks of no account to any landsman, of course, but even so, it makes for an amazing tapestry. The Indonesians are good people, too. Trustworthy. So there's plenty of opportunity for a businessman. I'm very fond of that part of the world, and I've got some excellent contacts there."

Oliver nodded. "Do you speak the language?"

"Which one?" Cuevas laughed. "I speak some Dutch, and smatterings of a few other local tongues, but there's a lot of different languages down there."

"I can imagine," Oliver said.

"As I remember, you're not a New Zealander," said Cameron.

"Heavens, no. The *Emma* is the fernleaf, not me. It's a lovely ship, strong as a bull, but Dunedin's not for me. That's where its owners are. My grandfather was from Bilbao, but I grew up in Dublin. I've spent so much time on the water, though, that I barely remember what nationality means any more. The sea is my nation now."

"Coming back to the ebony," Oliver said, "isn't it a rather long haul from the East Indies to here? Surely you could get a good price somewhere nearer."

Cuevas nodded. "Absolutely. But there's a huge demand for your iron and steel. So I load up with metals here, take them down to the East Indies, and come back with your ebony, and bundles of spices to fill the extra space. Heavy stuff, ebony."

"Certainly is," Cameron said. "Lovely. Nothing quite like it."

"It sounds like you've been doing the route for a while. Don't you already have someone lined up for your wood?" Oliver smiled at Cuevas to take any sting out of his question.

Scowling, Cuevas sighed. "I did. Unfortunately, he turned out to be a complete villain. The owners let themselves get suckered into extending him a line of credit, and we lost two full cargoes. He vanished, of course. That's the trouble with the land. Far too easy to hide. We pushed the police about it, but it didn't do any good. They didn't really care that a firm on the other side of the world had lost a boatload of money—literally—or that an

Irishman was trying to kick up a fuss. So from now on, I have strict orders. Half up front, half on delivery."

"I understand," said Oliver. "Excuse us a moment, would you?" He pulled his father away from the table.

Cameron looked impatient at the interruption. "What is it?"

"Honestly, Dad," Oliver sighed. "That man's no more a sea captain than I am."

What makes Oliver think that Frank Cuevas is a fraud?

HINT:
SHIP.

THE TIP

Mary Miller poured two cups of tea, and passed one across the table.

Jasmine Hillins took it gratefully and had a distracted sip. "It's not that anyone has complained, you understand."

"Of course," said Miss Miller.

"Word does get around though, doesn't it? To have a thief on the staff ..."

"Why don't you tell me about it from the beginning, my dear?"

Jasmine sighed. "Oh, Mary. I couldn't burden you like that."

"Nonsense. It's the least I can do."

"Well, if you insist ... Last Saturday, Hayden threw a little party for some of his pals from the club. There were maybe twenty of us in all, including the wives. As we

were saying goodbye to everyone, Mrs. Snell sent a message that she needed to see me immediately. I thought maybe there were problems with the following day's arrangements, but no. She'd caught a glimpse of one of the kitchen girls, Hailey Johnson, lurking in the pantry and tucking a large banknote into her purse. She called the girl over, and demanded to see her purse. Hailey turned it over sullenly, and there it was. Over a month's worth of her pay!"

"Shocking," Miss Miller said, suppressing the urge to ask how little Hayden paid the girl.

"Quite. I could hardly ask Hayden to call everyone and enquire as to whether they had been robbed of a substantial amount of money under our roof. Hailey insists that the note was tucked between pages 69 and 70 of a book which someone had placed on her tray. She says she didn't notice who it was, because she was busy collecting glasses. The wretched girl insists that it's a gift, a consideration from one of the gentlemen who didn't want to be spotted giving her a little something while his wife was around."

"Does she now?"

"I know! Of course, I'd hardly put it past some of Hayden's friends. Well, to be honest, I wouldn't entirely put it past any of them. Boys will be boys. But it's a very generous gift for just handing out the

champagne, if you know what I mean. There must be more to it than that."

"Yes. Did you have a look at the book in question?"

"Well, yes. It's a dreadful volume by some Irish fellow, full of blood and bodices and suspicious Eastern European noblemen. One of Hayden's. But it definitely is his copy, and it was clearly just taken from a bookshelf. There's no useful information to be gleaned there, I tell you."

"I see," said Miss Miller.

"Hayden's spoken to everyone without asking them directly, asked if they had a pleasant evening, that sort of thing, but no one seemed in the least bit put out. They all claim to have had an absolutely divine time, of course. None of them mentioned Hailey, either."

"Unfortunately, I think you may have to take this one at face value, Jasmine. Keep a careful eye on the girl, but unless someone speaks up, I don't see what else can be done."

Once Jasmine had gone, Miss Miller penned a short, anonymous note to Hailey Johnson:

I dare you deserved one little windfall, but I am watching. Steal anything again from the Hillins or their guests, and I'll drag you to the police station myself.

– Vigilant.

She sealed it, arranged to have it delivered discreetly, and went on about her business.

How does Miss Miller know that the money is stolen?

HINT:
BOOK.

THE CRYSTAL BALL

Oliver had to admit that Alicia's crystal ball was quite attractive. It was highly polished, of course, a sphere of smoky quartz some six inches in diameter. Cloudy flaws deep in the stone glittered in the candle-light, drawing the eye. However, whatever virtues the crystal ball may have possessed, it did not appear to convey any meaningful gift of second sight upon its owner who, almost as soon as she had sat down, whipped it out of her bag with a flourish and set it in front of herself on a cloth of mottled purple felt.

Adam winced at the sight of it, but held his tongue. He was far too polite a host to express his dismay. Ronnie grimaced, but he too kept quiet.

Mia felt no such compunctions, however. "Oh my word, Alicia. Surely we're not going to have to suffer more of your ridiculous quackery?"

Alicia's eyes narrowed. "I'd never expect you to understand, my dear. Scrying the future is a subtle art. This sphere was carved for the Maharaja of Chittagong three hundred years ago, for the use of his seers. It is imbued with delicate powers which only the most refined may access."

Come out of some flea-market for a pittance more like, Oliver thought to himself.

Mia snorted. "Perhaps you could gaze within and tell us how much longer this tiresome mystical phase of yours is going to last? You're no fun like this."

"I was awakened at Lammas," Alicia said stiffly. "There is no going back."

"Two weeks?" Mia sounded incredulous. "It feels more like two years."

"Fresh coffee?" Falsely jolly, Adam bustled round with a large pitcher, filling everyone's cups.

Oliver seized the moment of silence. "You must tell us about your hiking trip, Adam."

Smiling at him gratefully, Adam launched into a long and highly entertaining story of his misadventures in the hills the previous weekend. That led to a display of the wildflower specimens he'd brought back with him, and then Kira drew Alicia into a discussion about Renaissance art, and everything was back to normal.

The afternoon passed pleasantly after that. Adam ushered the group through into the dining room, where he served a late lunch of cold cuts and kept glasses filled. No one even stirred from the table until it was time to think about leaving. Oliver was getting ready to depart when a screech of outrage dragged everyone's attention back to the reception room. Inside, he found Alicia glaring around wildly.

"My orb! My orb is gone!"

"I'm sure it'll turn up," Oliver said soothingly, trying to stifle a yawn.

"Perhaps it has ascended to the spirit realm, to reunite with the Maharaja," Mia suggested from behind him.

Alicia shot her a filthy look.

Longingly eyeing the brimming pot of now-cold coffee on the reception-room table, Oliver helped Alicia to search the room. There was no sign of the crystal ball. Mightily disgruntled, she left, making it plain that she blamed Mia entirely.

A few minutes later, Oliver made his farewells. He thanked Adam for an entertaining time, and then fixed his friend with a firm look. "You're going to give it back to her, of course."

"What? I don't—" Adam's bluster faded as quickly as it had arrived under Oliver's calm gaze. "Oh, all right. Yes, of course I'll give it back. I was going to. She's been so tiresome the last few weeks, though. I couldn't resist the chance for a little prank."

"It'll pass. Remember her bee thing?"

Adam nodded glumly. "Only too well. But how the devil did you know, Olly?"

What made Oliver realize that Adam had taken the crystal ball?

HINT:
TABLE.

THE CAPTIVE

Rosalyn Reyes had been missing for three days, and when she was discovered, it was only by the thinnest thread of luck. Andrew Baum was an enthusiastic walker and knew much of the local countryside like the back of his hand. Taking a welcome day off from work, he decided to go for a hike in Easton woods and follow a trail he had not tried before. After walking for some time, he took a wrong turn and found himself at odds with his map.

He was about to retrace his steps when he realized that he could hear a very faint sound of someone crying. Following the sound led him to a clearing, in which stood a rickety shack. Inside, he discovered the missing young woman, uninjured, but chained securely to a pole. As soon as she was safe, the police put up a dragnet around that part of the woods and waited. Over the course of the afternoon, three men were apprehended in the area.

That was where the good luck ended. Miss Reyes knew nothing whatsoever about her captor. She had woken on the first day to find herself restrained and blindfolded, and had remained that way throughout. Not only had she not seen her captor, he had also refrained from touching her, and had only spoken

to her very minimally in a highly contrived hoarse whisper. Material found in the shack suggested that he was preparing a ransom demand to deliver to her parents, but again, there was nothing in it that would help identify the kidnapper. As a final blow, none of the three suspects had been carrying anything incriminating on their persons.

Inspector Parnacki smoothed out his moustache, fiddling with the ends irritably. He needed a lead suspect in order to justify an in-depth investigation. A stroll would help him to gather his thoughts, he decided. He packed a pipe, picked up the interview reports, and made his way to a local park.

Newton Stevens was an impecunious odd-job man who lived at Easton, a couple of miles from the woods. His transcript was quite irascible. "Of course I was in the woods. I'm always in the woods, ain't I? No crime to trap rabbits, leastways not last time I looked. I was going to check on my snares. Friday, ain't it? What else am I supposed to do on a Friday? Nothing, that's what, not since darned Adrian stopped work on that darned wall. Eh? Shack? Of course I don't live in a shack, you darned fool. It's a cabin, and it's in Easton. Shack indeed. You better turn me loose quickly, or so help me, I'll lose the light, and then it'll be boiled greens for dinner. No way for a man to live, boiled greens. Not without some rabbit."

Terence Moss worked at a drinking establishment in Easton. "I didn't do anything wrong," his transcript began. "You've got no right to arrest a man like that for just having a walk. If you worked in a bar like the Imperial, you'd want to get some peace and quiet of an afternoon yourself. I don't know what you're after, but you've got the wrong man. No opium, no hashish, I don't do any of that stuff. I haven't stolen anything since I was twelve. No, I don't recognize that shack. Never been near it. Don't even know where it is. Never seen that woman. I'd remember if anyone even slightly like that had ever been into the Imperial. Look, you know where I work and live. Just let me out of here, will you? I really can't afford to lose this job. I haven't done anything!"

Matthew Bird, finally, was a service engineer with a pipe-manufacturing company in Easton. "My last job had run long, so I decided to stroll in the woods while I had my packed lunch. Cheese and pickle sandwich. Very nice. I often do go for a little lunchtime walk, if it's been a tough morning. Nice to have a little break from it all, you know? My boss won't be very sympathetic about the amount of time this is taking now, however. I understand you're just doing your job, but surely we can get this sorted out swiftly. Why don't you put me in a line-up? I'd be delighted to … Well yes, of course, I want to be helpful. No, that shack doesn't look familiar, I'm afraid. Hardly seems the sort of place to develop steam-pipe problems. No, I'm afraid that girl doesn't look familiar either."

Parnacki tapped his pipe thoughtfully, and read over the transcripts again. His eyes brightened, and he turned to start back to the station.

Who has made Parnacki suspicious, and why?

HINT:
BLINDFOLD.

LAST WILL AND TESTAMENT

Ellie Williams was doing remarkably well, all things considered. Losing a beloved husband suddenly would have been difficult enough for any woman to cope with, but discovering that she was inexplicably cut out of his will was a hurtful insult to add to the shocking injury of his demise.

"It's not even the money," she said, tearfully.

Miss Miller gave Ellie's hand a squeeze.

"I just don't understand! Did I do something wrong? I can't imagine … Bob seemed happy. But he must have hated me!"

"I can't believe that, Ellie dear," Miss Miller said. "No one could hate you."

Ellie sniffed. "That's sweet of you, Mary. But obviously

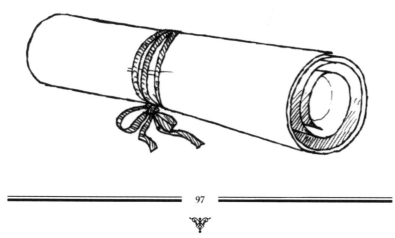

something was very, very wrong."

It was difficult to disagree. Bob Williams had suffered a heart attack in his sleep, not an entirely unusual fate for a well-fed man in his early sixties. A professor of English language and literature at the city's university, he had been comfortably tenured for years, and not much inclined to physical exertion. His will, however, had been something of a shock. It left his entire estate to the city's leading orchestra, with no provision whatsoever for his wife of twenty-five years. It made little sense. Williams had been reasonably enthusiastic about the orchestra's performances, but that seemed flimsy grounds to sign over one's worldly possessions to their funding drive.

"Where was the will located?" asked Miss Miller.

"In his office at the department," Ellie said. "I know what you're going to ask. All sorts of people have access, but it's Bob's handwriting. I can show you." She hurried off, and came back a moment later with the will in one hand and notes for a report in the other. The handwriting certainly seemed to match, and the will itself seemed straightforward.

I, Robert Alan Williams,
being of sound mind and judgment:
Do, of my own free will and accord, hereby record my last will and
testament, fully and explicitly revoking any and all preceeding
testaments in every particular.
I hereby bequeath all my earthly possessions and residuary estate,

including such parts as may fall after the lapse of my living interests, in entirety, to the City Chamber Orchestra, from now into perpetuity.

Then there was the usual date and signature. Miss Miller tapped her chin thoughtfully. "Yes, I see what you mean. The penmanship certainly does look the same. Were there any signs that he was getting … vague?"

Shaking her head, Ellie said, "He'd been feeling a bit under the weather for a while, but he was still as sharp as a pin."

"Under the weather?"

"Just some sort of persistent bug. A bit of malaise. Nothing serious."

"You don't know if he had any enemies, do you?"

Ellie looked startled by that. "Enemies? An English professor? I hardly think so. Academia can be quite spiteful, and he had rivals—there are always people waiting impatiently for tenured slots to become available—but no, none of them were important enough to label as enemies."

Miss Miller sighed, and gave Ellie's hand another squeeze. "I'm afraid you may be wrong there, my dear. The will is a clear fake, and I very much fear that Bob was murdered."

Why does Miss Miller think the will is a fake?

HINT:
WILL.

THE MISSING MURDERER

Inspector Parnacki strolled around the large parking area, puffing on his pipe. The object of his annoyance, a small, tattered truck, was parked towards the middle of the space.

"It doesn't make sense, Inspector." Damon Olivers was the night clerk from a small grocery that looked onto the lot.

Keeping his irritation well disguised, Parnacki turned back to the man. "You're sure about the order of events?"

"Yes, of course."

"Talk me through it one more time, would you?"

Olivers nodded. "I was doing the evening sweep and tidy. It's usually quiet at this time, so that's when I get to sweep the floors, stock the shelves, throw out anything that's gone bad, and so on. I was down by the flour, trying to clean up a small spill from one of the bags. I heard a huge bang, and everything rattled. Clouds of flour drifted down, which made me curse, I can tell you."

"I'm sure," said Parnacki.

"Almost immediately, I heard whistles. I went up to the front of the shop and saw a huge cloud of smoke, with the truck in the middle of it. The door to Berrits, the tailor's shop, was swinging closed. I saw a couple of police officers running.

There were shots from Berrits. I could hear them through the walls. One of the officers pulled out a gun and returned fire. Then everything was chaos for a while. Lots of shouting, and shooting, and whistles. I was on the floor behind the counter by then. I expect you know the rest from your men."

"Indeed I do. And you're confident that there's no back exit from Berrits?"

"Definitely not. All our units are the same. Big shop area, small back room, tiny rest room. Nothing else. The only way in or out is through the shop. Well, unless you break a wall down, I suppose."

Parnacki shook his head. "Everything appears intact."

"So does this mean whoever did this has got away?"

"Thank you for your time, Mr. Olivers. You've been very helpful."

Olivers nodded, with a wry grin. "I'll be in the shop tidying for another half hour if you need me, inspector. Good luck."

Parnacki left the grocery and made his way over to the truck. Officer Christopher Coleridge watched him approach. He had been the first man on the scene, and still looked shaky.

"Hello again, Inspector," Coleridge said.

"Good evening, Officer Coleridge. I know it's tiresome but would you summarize events for me one last time?"

"I heard an explosion and came running. Lee was with me, and I could hear that another patrol was close by. I recognized the truck as a bank transport, and assumed that the blast was someone trying to blow the safe, so I readied my pistol. As I approached the truck, shots were fired from the third unit in the row of shops. I returned fire. Several other officers arrived and provided assistance. When it became clear that there was no more gunfire coming from the unit, we stopped shooting and called for the weapon to be thrown out. There was no response and after several minutes I went into the shop, calling for the gunman to lie flat as I advanced. A pistol was on the floor near the front window, and the driver of the truck was lying on the floor at the back of the room, handcuffed and facing away from the door. He had been shot through the back of the head. There was no sign of the murderer. We searched absolutely everywhere."

"And there's no way the murderer could have come out of the front door in the confusion?"

"No, sir. I had my eyes on that door the whole time from the first shot until the moment we went in."

Parnacki nodded. "I am quite sure you did, officer. Thank you. I suspect I know where he is."

Where is the gunman?

HINT:
VICTIM.

UNNY BUSINESS

Oliver James had met Rory Hays in an Italian Renaissance Architecture class and the pair had been firm friends ever since, so there was nothing odd about Rory inviting him round one afternoon. What seemed less regular was Rory's request that Oliver be on his guard for, as he put it, "signs of funny business."

Oliver had been chatting for a while with Rory and his fiancée Sabrina when the doorbell rang. "Ah, good," Rory said, and headed for the door. He came back a few moments later with a tall, dignified man in his mid-20s. "Kier, I'd like you to meet my fiancée, Sabrina Firman, and this is Oliver James, a dear friend from my college days. We first met in a class on Renaissance building design in the Italian north-east. Sabrina, Olly, this is Kier Jones. We've been working together for six months now. He's a technical genius. He may even be a wizard."

"Rory is far too kind," Kier said. "It is a pleasure to meet you both."

Sabrina smiled. "I believe we met briefly at your offices back in the summer, Mr. Jones. Rory was showing off the miniatures for the Crown development."

"Ah, yes, quite possibly," Kier said. "Forgive me. I was somewhat distracted."

"Fretting over the quantity of slate we were going to need, if I recall," Rory said.

Laughing, Kier nodded. "It is an awful lot of the stuff. You're also an architect, Mr. James?"

"Call me Oliver, please. And yes, as much as possible. I do all my father's design work at the moment, but there are certain other responsibilities that he keeps trying to foist on me as well."

"I'll fetch the coffee," Sabrina said. She rose gracefully and left the room.

"I understand your predicament," Kier told Oliver. "My own father and I do not see entirely eye to eye. He feels that I should be safely married by now and presenting him with grandchildren. I'm not entirely sure what the hurry is."

"Parents are sent to bedevil us," Rory said. "Once they're through being horribly embarrassing, My father once turned that is.

up at school with a toy duck I'd left at home—quite deliberately, too. He just waltzed into the classroom without a care in the world, holding up the blasted thing and making quacking noises. He marched straight over to my desk, quacking, and presented the duck to me with all the solemnity of a king conveying a knighthood. Then he turned on his heel and marched out again. I was seven. As I'm sure you can imagine, all my schoolfriends quacked at me incessantly for the next year or more."

"It's no wonder you turned out the way you did," Sabrina said, coming back into the room with a tray. "Mad as a loon."

"I'm not mad, damn it," said Rory, pretending apoplectic fury. "I'm misunderstood."

Oliver clapped him on the shoulder. "She understands you all too well, old chap."

Grinning, Sabrina said, "Oliver, how do you take your coffee again?"

"Just cream, thank you."

"Of course." She prepared his coffee and passed it over, handing the other two their own drinks. "I thought that was it, but one can never be too careful."

"Wish someone had told my father that once or twice," Rory said. "I still can't stand to be closed in a room with a duck to this very day."

"Does that ever prove inconvenient?" Kier looked at Rory curiously.

"No," Rory said. "Never, in fact. I don't much mingle in duck-fancier's circles. But I live in hope."

"I'll see what I can do," Oliver said. "I know a chap who breeds mallards. I dare say he'd lend me a roomful of the blighters to toss you into."

Rory groaned. "Et tu, you brute?"

Some highly congenial hours later, Rory saw Oliver to the door. "So—" he began.

"Let me guess," Oliver said quietly. "You suspect Sabrina and Kier of carrying on together behind your back."

Rory nodded, suddenly miserable.

"Well, for what it's worth, I'd be surprised if either of them would do that to you. They do both seem genuinely fond of you. But—and I want to emphasize that this could be perfectly innocent—she knows him well, and is desperately trying to pretend otherwise."

Why would Oliver come to that conclusion?

HINT:
ETIQUETTE.

THE SALESMAN'S WIFE

In the morning light, the footsteps were readily visible in the wet ground. The imprints of heavy size eleven shoes led from the street across the ground in front of the house to a tree-stump, milled around a bit, and then made a line straight to the front door, where they met the stone path from the main gate and vanished. Inspector Parnacki followed them cautiously, keeping away from the tracks so that his own prints didn't interfere with them. The spare front door key was nestled inside the stump's hollow. Puffing on his pipe, he went back to the house.

Douglas Chatman, the victim's husband, was standing on the front porch. An average size at his best, he looked small and shrunken in on himself now, and there was a grey tinge to his skin.

"I understand you were out of the city last night, sir," Parnacki said to him.

Nodding, Chatman said, "Yes. I'm a salesman, and I work across the region. It means I spend a lot of time on the road. Melina didn't like me being away so much, but there never seemed to be any option. If I'd found another job …" He stifled a sob. "I was in Soutton yesterday. I have receipts, of course. I should have pressed on home. If I'd been here, maybe she'd still be alive."

"I find it best not to second-guess the past," said Parnacki, gently. "Perhaps you would both have perished."

Chatman shuddered.

"In your initial statement, you told the officer that the murderer must have used the spare key to gain access."

"Yes," Chatman said. "The house was locked when I arrived. There was no sign of damage anywhere, and Melly's key was in her purse. We never advertised the spare key, but we never took any particular pains to hide it either. God alive, we were such fools."

"There are no other keys?"

"No. Just mine, Melly's, and the spare. We used the spare fairly often. If Melly went out without her bag—to see a friend briefly, or something—she'd just use the spare without a second thought. Anyone keeping an eye on the house might have known about it."

"You're quite certain about this?"

"Of course," Chatman said.

Parnacki nodded. "Were friends or family told about the key?"

"Only Melly's parents."

"I see," Inspector Parnacki said. "Can you think of any reason why someone might have wanted to kill your wife?"

Chatman shook his head. "Absolutely not. She was a lovely woman, charming and outgoing. The last year had been quite hard on her, but she had plenty of friends, and so far as I know, not a rival or enemy in the world. It must have been some sort of depraved maniac. I can't imagine anything else."

"There are certainly some unpleasant characters at large in the world," Parnacki said. "However, in this case, I do not think that we need to start a manhunt for a murderer with size eleven feet."

Chatman stared at him. "No?"

"No. Douglas Chatman, I'm afraid that I am going to have to ask you to accompany me to the police station."

Why does Parnacki suspect Chatman?

HINT:
THE STUMP.

THE NARCISSIST

Inspector Parnacki tapped the stem of his pipe thoughtfully against his palm. Aiden Pearce had been unusually unpopular, even among murder victims. A crashingly narcissistic bore with poorly managed criminal tendencies, he had generally operated on the right side of the law—enough so that the police had never been able to charge him with anything, anyway. When informed of his death, his young wife had burst into tears of relieved joy, much to the officer's discomfort. Parnacki decided to interview her first.

Annabeth Pearce had regained her composure when Parnacki met her. Slender and twenty-two, Annabeth had slightly bulging eyes which gave her the appearance of a perpetually startled doe.

"I feel I must apologize for what I did this morning," she told him. "I know it is unseemly to speak ill of the dead, but my husband was exhausting to be married to, and often prone to terrifying moments of rage. He would never have let me go. When I heard the news, it felt as if my soul had been set free."

Parnacki nodded politely. "Of course. Can you think of anyone who would have wanted to kill him?"

Annabeth laughed bitterly. "Anyone who'd spent more than five minutes in his company?"

"Quite. Anyone specific?"

"No more so than usual," Annabeth said. "Not that I know of."

"I'm sure you understand that I have to ask where you were between 7.30 and 8.30 this morning."

She nodded. "I was at the market, buying food and other necessaries. Everything had to be purchased fresh every morning, in case he came home for lunch, and then again in the afternoon, for dinnertime. The wastage was staggering. There are several stallholders I shop from every day who can confirm I was there."

Michael Solis, Aiden's assistant, was in his early thirties. He was a wary, tired-looking man, prematurely balding, with a sallow cast to his skin.

"I found the body, yes," Solis told Parnacki. "Pearce always got in before 7.30. The rest of us were under strict instructions not to arrive before 8.30. He liked an hour in the morning to work privately. I immediately knew he was dead. He was slumped face down over his desk, blood pooling out over everything."

Parnacki nodded. "Can you think of anyone who might have wanted to murder Mr. Pearce?"

"He was a self-obsessed cheat and bully," Solis said. "Never popular traits, and particularly not in a freewheeling trader. Personally I loathed him, but his death is inconvenient—I'll have to find another job. I was at home with my fiancée until 8.10, as always, and then I came straight here."

Anthony Stewart was Pearce's bookkeeper. Tall and thin, and a few years older than Solis, he had something of a librarian about him. When he spoke, it was with a precise, almost clipped accent.

"You must understand that I knew little of Mr. Pearce's actual business," Stewart said. "He generated a layer of obfuscation in order to avoid his subordinates gaining enough information to facilitate a betrayal. It's a shame, actually. I would have liked to have had a look at the shipping manifest he was working on."

"So you don't know of any specific

enemy Mr. Pearce may have had?"

"I'm afraid not, no. He left lots of unhappy people in his wake. As for my movements, I was at home until 8.20 before arriving here at 8.45, as my wife will attest."

The final employee, Noah Parham, worked as a general office junior. Young and heavily muscled, Parham compensated for his lack of education with a hearty cheerfulness. He seemed utterly unbothered by the morning's events. "Someone finally got the old dog," he said. "It was going to happen sooner or later. He wasn't very nice."

"Any idea who?" asked Parnacki.

"Lord, no. Could be anyone, really. No one had made any open threats recently that I'd heard of."

"And where were you from 7.30 this morning?"

"At the docks," Parham said. "Delivering a package. There's plenty there as will vouch for that."

Once Parham had left, Inspector Parnacki leant back in his chair. "Nice and straightforward," he said to himself.

Who does Parnacki suspect?

HINT:
PAPERWORK.

THE COTTON FIRE

"It's a blow, Olly." Benjamin Avila looked tired, and there were still smears of ash under his fingernails. "The fire destroyed a lot of stock. It leaves me in a precarious position, and the insurance people have already made it clear that if it was an avoidable accident that started it, they won't cover me."

Oliver grimaced sympathetically. "Do you have any idea how it happened?"

"One of the tailors was in there, a chap named Darman. He said that the roller on the door had worn down to the metal, and when he slid the door open, it sparked against the stone. Some of the sparks landed in a bundle of cotton nearby, and everything went up. He tried to stamp out the fire, but it spread too quickly. He had to get out."

"I see."

Benjamin nodded. "I don't really understand how it could happen, but it sounds very avoidable to me, which means I'm in big trouble. Look, I'd never ask you to do anything underhanded, you know that. But you've got a good eye for details, and if those stories you've been telling me are true, you've got a nose for mischief as well. It's not that I distrust Darman exactly, but

… well, he hasn't been with me long, and the industry has been a bit more cut-throat than I'm comfortable with recently. If it's my fault for not maintaining the door properly, fine and well, I'll take it on the chin. Could you just make sure that there's not something else afoot?"

"Of course, Benj. I'd be happy to have a poke around. Lead on."

Benjamin vanished for a few moments before returning with a tidy, well-built man in his late twenties. "Mr. Darman, this is Oliver James. He's helping me with the insurance report. Oliver, this is Ryder H. Darman, the tailor who was in the fabric room at the time of the fire."

"Nice to meet you, Mr. Darman," Oliver said as they shook hands. "Could you tell me what happened?"

"Happy to help, sir. The door of the fabric room had been making an unhealthy grating noise for a week or two. I figured it was the hinges what was doing it, and didn't pay it no mind. I headed back there looking for some velvet silks, and when I went in, sure enough, the door scraped nastily as I slid it open. I looked down, and saw sparks coming from the floor. Next thing I know, they'd got into the raw cotton, and it went up like a fireball. I tried to put it out, but it was already spreading. All I could do was run for it."

Oliver scratched at a small itch on his jawline. "I see. Thank you."

Benjamin nodded, and Darman strode off back to his station.

"Let's have a look at this door, then," Oliver said.

"This way," said Benjamin. He sounded glum.

When they got to the fabric room, Oliver could see just how much damage had been done. The place was four-fifths empty, with scorch-marks still staining the walls and the concrete floor. There was no loose stock in the room, just a few large bags. The door had suffered in the fire, warping visibly. It was still soot-blackened.

Oliver knelt to have a look at the rollers. What coating they may have possessed had been burnt away in the blaze, so that only the naked bronze remained. It was impossible to guess what state they had been in before. The track that they rolled in was bare concrete, cut straight into the floor. He straightened back up, and pushed at the door thoughtfully. It still folded up successfully, but shrieked horribly as it moved.

"Was it normal for there to be cotton near the door?"

"It's not uncommon," Benjamin replied. "I didn't think to suggest that it should be put further back, and we don't have specific locations for different types of stock. Too much variety in the levels we need to carry from week to week." He sighed. "It seems cut and dried, doesn't it. I suppose I'll just have to face the music like a man."

"Not at all," Oliver said. "You should call the police."

Why does Oliver suspect arson?

HINT:
DOOR.

THE MISSING VALUABLES

"Please forgive the mess." Marilyn Hunt waved a hand around helplessly. "We have builders in the place, and although one would think that they would confine themselves to the area they're working on, they seem to have an endless talent for spreading disruption everywhere."

The library was certainly in quite a state. Several bookcases had been pulled from the wall, and random shelves seemed to have been stripped, their books piled up haphazardly on the floor.

Miss Miller gave Marilyn a smile. "Don't mention it, my dear. I know how these things can be."

"It's just so random," Marilyn said. "Yesterday afternoon, we lost power to the kitchen. It was a disaster. Mrs. Dixon was beside herself. The night before, it was the entire east wing, the lodge, and the guest annexe, for almost an hour. The day before that, the ballroom filled with a nasty purple smoke that smelled like chickens, and just wouldn't go away."

"What on earth are they doing for you?"

"Shoring up the foundations. Most of the time, they're in the basement banging away like furious drummers, but they crop up all over the place, as they find various trouble-spots. I'd be at my wits' end even without the theft."

Miss Miller took a sip of her tea. "Do tell me about that, Marilyn."

"It was the case containing my mother's old valuables. I wear bits from there sometimes, to remember her. The case is in my dressing room. It never moves. Except, the night before last, it wasn't there when I got ready for bed. I remember noticing it after dinner, so it must have been taken between eight and ten." Marilyn heaved a sigh.

"Who else was in the house?"

"Donald, obviously, but I think we can rule him out. My husband may be odd, but he's not that odd. Wednesday. Hmm. The builders had all gone. So had Mrs. Dixon. Bailey and the new girl, Edna I think, they were both here. Donald's nephew, Ellis, is staying with us, but he was out with friends until late."

"I could have a word with them," Miss Miller said. "See if anyone noticed anything?"

"Oh, would you?" Marilyn smiled. "I know you've got a keen nose for that sort of thing."

Bailey, the butler, was an austere-looking man of medium height and grave aspect. He appeared to be in his late forties,

but he held himself rigorously upright. He'd
been with Marilyn and Donald for years,
and although he'd met Miss Miller dozens
of times, he remained as professionally
distant as a perfect stranger.

"Good afternoon, Bailey,"
Miss Miller said, once
Marilyn had sent him in.

"Ma'am," he replied,
utterly noncommittal as to the
quality of his or anyone else's
day.

"I wonder, did you notice
anything odd on Wednesday
evening, after dinner?"

Bailey's gaze flickered
momentarily, as clear an expression of
surprise as Miss Miller had ever seen from the man. There was a
moment's pause. "Odd, Ma'am?"

"Anyone skulking around, windows left open, that sort of
thing."

"No, Ma'am."

"Where were you at that time?"

"In my workroom," he said, stiffly.

"Very good, Bailey." Miss Miller smiled at him warmly.

He nodded, offered one last "Ma'am," and left again.

Edna Reeves was a vivacious teenager with an irrepressible smile. "No, I never saw anything odd-looking," she said. "Not that it's my place to say what's odd or not. I was down in the kitchens, cleaning up after dinner like I always does. That Mrs. Dixon is a wonderful cook, mind, but it seems to me that cooking is a really messy business. Sometimes it seems to take three large pans to just boil an egg. I was down there until gone eleven."

Ellis Hunt, finally, was a pleasant-seeming young man in his late twenties. "Sorry, Miss Miller," he said. "I wasn't in the main house on Wednesday evening. I was playing poker with friends from six until Lord knows when in the morning. We use a room in the lodge that faces away from the main house, so there's no view. Even if we'd been in the dining room, though, I doubt I'd have noticed anything. The evening went by in a flash."

When Ellis had taken his leave, Marilyn returned. "Any luck, Mary?" She seemed equal parts concerned and optimistic.

"I'm afraid I've got a rather strong suspicion, yes," Miss Miller said.

Who does Miss Miller suspect, and why?

HINT:
TIMING.

THE CARTOGRAPHER

J ack Chamberlain's eccentricity was well-known. A passionate cartographer, he spent every available hour making incredibly detailed maps of places that had never existed, one after another. Each was precisely as large as his expansive dining-table would allow, and they remained on that hallowed surface from their very first mark to the moment of their completion, a week or more later. They ranged from the global to the extremely local in scale. It was difficult to say whether all the maps illustrated the same non-existent world, or whether each one was entirely separate. Inspector Parnacki wasn't entirely convinced that it mattered either way, and since Chamberlain had been bludgeoned to death with a paperweight somewhere around 4.30pm on Saturday afternoon, he wasn't telling.

Several people had been at Chamberlain's house that day. Parnacki decided to start by interviewing them, to see what the victim's last hours had been like.

Bruno Marks was Chamberlain's brother-in-law. An easygoing man well into middle age, he was dressed casually in slacks and a button-down shirt. If he felt any unease at being in an interview room, it was very well hidden. "The famous

Paddington Parnacki," Marks said, when the Inspector introduced himself. "It's a privilege, Inspector."

"Thank you for coming," Inspector Parnacki replied, impassively. "You're married to Jack Chamberlain's sister, I believe?"

"That's right. Ashley. We've been married for twelve years."

"Did you know Jack well?"

"I'm not sure anyone did, honestly. He lived inside his own head. Always had."

"When was the last time you saw him?"

Marks sighed. "I saw him on Saturday afternoon. I wanted to talk to him about a financial opportunity. We'd done some similar business in the past, quite profitably. I arrived a little after three. Jack was poring over one of his half-completed doodles when I arrived, and after he'd had his ritual moan about being interrupted, we had a useful discussion. I wasn't there more than half an hour."

"What was the nature of this opportunity?"

"A project I'm in the process of starting," Marks said. "Property development."

"I see," Parnacki said. "I appreciate your time, Mr. Marks."
Wyatt Torres had been Chamberlain's gardener. Tall and
strongly built, he had a weathered face that made him look
substantially older than his actual age of thirty-two. "I
worked that garden for a dozen years," he said. "I know her
inside and out. Mr. Jack was a private man, in his way. Very
informal and easy to please, but you never saw below the
surface layers."

"You were at Mr. Chamberlain's house on
Saturday?"

"That I was—twelve to two Saturdays, Mondays
and Wednesdays, regular as clockwork."

"How was Mr. Chamberlain that day?"

"I didn't talk to him. I only talk to him on
Mondays, to confirm what I'm doing that week. He
doesn't much like being disturbed when he's working.
But I saw him through the windows a few times later
on, pacing up and down. That usually meant he was
having a bad day of it."

Chamberlain's housekeeper, Hailey Laramie, was
a petite woman in her late twenties. "He was lovely
most of the time," she told Parnacki. "He could get
moody, when something went wrong, but it wasn't
common. He seemed fine when I arrived on Saturday
morning, beavering away putting some ruins into the
middle of a patch of woodland. My routine was to get

in mid-morning, do a bit of tidying, and prepare a hot lunch and heatable dinner for him. So I'm gone by 12:30. Mondays was all-day, with the main clean and tidy, and the weekly shopping. Bit like having a greying teenage son, really. He wasn't someone you got close to, if you know what I mean, but I'll miss him."

The only other person who had seen Chamberlain that day was a young delivery man, Tristan Turner, who worked for an art supplies store. "I was delivering a bundle of cartridge paper, custom-cut and individually rolled. I was running a bit late, because we'd been waiting on a stock shipment, so I got there about 12:45. Mr. Chamberlain was usually okay, but he was in a filthy mood on Saturday. He waved around a crumpled, coffee-stained wad the size of a football, and yelled at me that I'd destroyed Hookland Point. I couldn't think what he meant at first, then I realized it was a map he'd been working on so I apologized. He took his delivery and I left. That's it, I'm afraid." He hesitated a moment. "That's pretty mild, for a delivery. Didn't bother me in the slightest. I'd never hurt a fly, me."

Parnacki thanked Turner for his time, promised to be in touch, and walked back to his office, packing fresh tobacco into his pipe. "Time to investigate that liar," he muttered to himself.

Who does Parnacki suspect of lying, and why?

HINT:
MAP.

HENDRICKS IN THE FRAME

Miss Miller smiled. "It's lovely to see you again, Mr. Hendricks. To what do I owe the pleasure?"

Clayton Hendricks smoothed his bushy beard nervously. "After that horrible Mattingley affair … That is, Miss Miller, I'm in some trouble, and I hoped you might be able to assist me. It's not of my own making, I swear."

"I'd be happy to try. Please, take a seat. Would you like some tea? Shoo, Aubrey." Gently pushing her cat off the spare chair, she rang for a fresh pot of tea. "Why don't you tell me the nature of your problem?"

"Thank you," Hendricks said gratefully. "Have I mentioned that I'm a wood merchant?"

"In the August issue of the Ornithological Society journal four years ago, yes."

Hendricks blinked. "Ah, good. So, I agreed to provide some lumber for a construction project not far from the city. The Lawrence development."

Miss Miller nodded.

"I was there two days ago, discussing the next shipment with the site's foreman. They've been stuck waiting for materials for a week or more, and it looks like it's ongoing. They were just putting

---

protective tarpaulin over the frame when I got there, against the storm that's supposed to hit tonight. I'm going to be able to help them with some of their requirements, but it's more than just wood they need. Several of their suppliers have dropped them recently, so they're in a bit of a bind.

Anyway, while I was there, someone stole the entire collection of plans from the site office. The chief architect is utterly enraged, as you can imagine. But a witness has come forward identifying me as the thief, and even if they don't push a criminal charge, they're threatening to destroy me financially. I've never stolen a thing in my life. But it's my word against his. I don't know what to do. Do you have any advice?"

"Hm. It certainly sounds horrible, my dear. Maybe you'd provide me with the details?"

As Clayton described it, the site was still barely formed. Foundations had been set in place, along with most of the primary supporting timbers, but nothing else. "It's just a skeleton of a house right now," he told her.

Having entered the site, he had parked near the storage depot, and spent some minutes unloading stock. Next had come a meeting with the foreman, whom he had finally found in the workers' break room.

"Was he alone in there?" Miss Miller asked.

"Lord, no," Clayton said. "There must have been a dozen men in there. It was too busy to talk shop. We came out and made our way round to the site office, which is on the far side of the skeleton. They have some lovely jays up there, bold as brass. I went into the office, and we hammered out a deal for some more shipments. Then we left again. The foreman went back to work, and I went home."

"Hm," Miss Miller said. "And I assume someone says differently?"

"One of the builders. He says that he was just about to go into the break room when he saw the foreman and me leave the site office. Then, apparently, I doubled back as soon as the foreman was out of the way, vanished back inside for a minute, and came back out stuffing something up the front of my shirt. So he went to check, discovered the plans missing, and ran to alert the foreman."

Miss Miller smiled suddenly. "That's wonderful."

Clayton looked uncertainly at her. "How so?"

"We can go to the foreman this instant, and clear your name. I suspect he'll want to call the police."

What has Miss Miller discovered?

HINT:
LINE.

THE GARDENER

Ian Page had been killed some time on Saturday afternoon. His daughter, Hannah, had been there for lunch with her children before departing around 3pm. He was discovered shortly after 7pm by an old friend, Atticus Glenn, and had been dead for at least two hours. Neither visitor was a suspect. Glenn had been golfing all afternoon in the company of three other men. Hannah had left Page's house and gone straight to visit her sister, Ellie, and the two families had spent the rest of the day together.

Inspector Parnacki stroked the stem of his pipe thoughtfully. Page had lived alone, and had done since the death of his wife some eight years earlier. He had owned a modest house in a quiet suburb of the city and spent much of his time working in his garden. The generous front lawn was broken up by attractively arranged flowerbeds and enclosed by tall dark hedges trimmed with exacting precision. A small fountain burbled water into a well-kept ornamental pond. The back of the property was mostly given over to vegetables—rows of beans, tomatoes and soft fruit. There was also a small greenhouse that looked as if it were primarily for cultivation rather than housing exotic plants.

The inside of the house was comfortably tidy, with a preponderance of personal ornaments of no particular value to the world at large. Page had been struck down in his sitting room, apparently from behind, with a common garden shovel. So far as Parnacki had been able to ascertain, Page had no significant debts, no particular wealth, and, in fact, no financial dealings of any interest whatsoever. His daughters characterized him as independent and quiet, content to just enjoy his home and garden.

Parnacki was strolling around the front garden thoughtfully when he heard the front gate swing open. A police officer came into view, followed by a bald, well-dressed man in his sixties. The pair made their way over.

"Inspector, you should talk to this gentleman. He may have seen someone yesterday!" The officer seemed excited.

Parnacki brightened. "Thank you, officer." He turned to the man. "My name is Parnacki. I'm investigating the events surrounding Mr. Page's death."

"The name's Moody. Sam. I live next door, at number 56."

"Did you know Mr. Page well?"

"Not especially," Moody said. "I knew Ian well enough to say hello to, and we were on decent terms, but he wasn't a friend. He was the quiet type. Self-sufficient."

"I understand," Parnacki said. "And what was it you saw yesterday?"

"I had to go out yesterday afternoon, for some milk. I was halfway to my gate when I saw a young man crossing Ian's lawn. He had a spade with him, so I assumed Ian needed some help shifting some earth, but there was something about the way he was walking that made me suspicious. I watched him go up to the door and then slip inside. That's why I can still remember him clearly. Barely more than twenty he was, with a brutish cast to his face. Clean-shaven, sullen-looking, a wine-stain blotch on his left cheek. He was wearing dark homespun trousers and an off-white shirt. Oh, and a cap. Looked like someone used to hard physical work."

"Do you remember what his cap was like?"

"A loud check pattern. Quite stood out, it did."

Parnacki nodded. "Indeed it would. Officer, please place Mr. Moody under arrest for the murder of Ian Page."

Why does Parnacki suspect Moody?

HINT:
GARDEN.

DOBSON'S LEATHERWORKS

Kelly Saylor was doing an excellent job of containing her distress. In her place, Oliver James thought that he would probably have been a gibbering wreck.

"I'm extremely sorry for your loss, Miss Saylor. I'm not sure how I can help you, though."

She shrugged wearily. "You designed the Dobson Leatherworks for your father's company to construct."

"Surely you don't suspect me of murdering your father."

"No, no, of course not. But you know the place better than anyone. You might be able to spot something …" She trailed off helplessly.

Oliver sighed. "I remember the project. Three years ago. Trying to find a location where we could get permission for a tannery and still get river access for the runoff was a total nightmare. That's why it's down past Burton. But it's not as if I memorized every flat-plan I ever laid out." He paused, looking at the misery of her expression. "I suppose there might be something I remember, though. Why not start from the beginning?"

She gave him a brief, grateful smile. "I told you that my father worked for Jack Dobson, didn't I? He was one of the

financial administrators for the Leatherworks. A week ago, he
discovered some worrying discrepancies, both in the books and
the stocks. He took the matter to Jack, and was basically waved
away. Well, my father wasn't the kind who backed down when
he was sure he was correct. So he started investigating. Four
evenings ago, when I had dinner with him, he told me that he'd
managed to confirm his initial findings, concrete evidence of
systemic abuse. He said that he was going to confront Dobson
after work the next day. He never came home."

"That must have been horrifying," Oliver said.

Kelly nodded. "I got hold of the police
the following
morning. They
said they'd keep
a look out. Two
days later—
yesterday
afternoon—
his body
turned up in
that reeking
river that
runs down
the side of the
Leatherworks.
The police

estimated that he'd been dead for eighteen hours, so since Sunday evening. They were reluctant to confront Dobson, unsurprisingly. He's got a lot of clout."

"Dobson is a powerful man," Oliver said.

"I managed to push the police into enquiring in the end, but the slimy toad can prove that he was over fifty miles away all weekend, in the company of a large group of friends and relatives. He claims he fired Dad on Friday afternoon, because he'd become irrational. Then the police found that Dad's stomach was full of whiskey. Now they're saying that he must have gone to drown his sorrows on Friday night, and just stayed out drinking until he fell in the river and drowned on Sunday night some time. But Dad wasn't much of a drinker, and he hated whiskey. This whole thing stinks. I'm sure he caught Dobson committing fraud, and Dobson killed him. I just can't see how, and the police are too scared of the man to investigate more deeply without a good reason. His alibi is perfect."

Oliver took her hand excitedly. "No, don't you see? It's no good!"

What is wrong with Dobson's alibi?

HINT:
RIVER.

THE BRIDEGROOM

There was something particularly unpleasant about being murdered on your wedding day, Inspector Parnacki thought. The victim, Joseph McNeill, had been killed by a heavy blow to the back of the head on the morning of the ceremony. His corpse was found seated in one of the chairs in his room, fully dressed, and with a freshly cut pink rose in his buttonhole. The only obvious sign of disorder was a bloody smear on the wall near the door. No murder weapon was in sight.

McNeill and his closest friends—the best man and the ushers—had booked into the Empire Hotel the night before. The hotel manager had been only too happy to lend Parnacki a room for initial interviews. The bride and her party were in the Grand, on the far side of the church from the Empire.

"We'll start with the groom's party," Parnacki told his assisting officer, a newly promoted detective named Raul Venegas.

Venegas nodded crisply. "The best man is Keith Milton. I'll call him."

Milton was a pleasant-looking man in his mid-twenties. He

was still dressed in his wedding outfit, a dark morning suit with a deep silver vest and cravat, and a crisp white shirt. He was very pale, and seemed somewhat dazed. Parnacki greeted him gently, and asked him about the events of the morning.

"They told me Joe was dead," he said. "I don't understand."

"Did Joe have any enemies?" Parnacki asked.

"Of course not. That's such a melodramatic word. Who has enemies?"

"Rivals, then. Anyone angry with him?"

Milton shook his head. "No. He'd have told me." He shuddered. "I suppose there must be. But I don't know about it. He was an actuary. Not the type to inspire murder."

"What was the routine this morning?"

"We all met for breakfast at 7.30 sharp—that's Joe,

Parker, Gage and I. We had a few drinks last night, so there were some sore heads, but nothing serious. Around 8.15, we went back to our rooms to start getting ready. At 10.00, I met Gage and Parker downstairs as arranged, but Joe wasn't there. Gage went to check on him at 10.15, and he … That is, he found the body."

"You were in your room from 8.15 to 10.00?"

"Of course, but I don't see how I could prove it. We all had separate rooms. I went looking for some ice at around 8.45, but I didn't see anyone, and I didn't call in on any of the guys."

"That's all for now," Parnacki told him. "Thank you, Mr. Milton."

Next up was Parker Newman, the brother of the bride, Kimberly. He was a tall, slender man with dark eyes, also wearing his formal outfit. He looked every bit as pale and shaky as Keith Milton had done.

"We met up in the hotel dining room early, for breakfast. I had a bit of a headache, but it was a good atmosphere. Then Joe never showed at 10.00. Eventually, Gage went to look." He sighed heavily. "Kim will be completely devastated. This is a terrible, terrible blow to us all." He rubbed absently at a spot of blood on his right forefinger, then noticed Parnacki's curiosity. "I stabbed myself with a pin when I was fixing my cravat."

"Can you think of anyone who might have wanted to cause Joe harm?"

Newman thought for a moment. "No. I can't imagine anyone

wanting to kill him. He wasn't super-rich, he wasn't a jerk, he wasn't a crook. He was just nice and funny, and my sister loved him more than anyone in the world."

"Where were you between breakfast and 10am?" Parnacki asked.

"In my room," Parker said. "Getting dressed slowly and carefully. Well, as carefully as I could manage with a hangover, anyway."

Gage Osborne had been friends with McNeill and Milton since high school. He was strongly built and he, too, was wearing the same suit, shirt and cravat outfit as the other men. There was an unhealthy pallor to his skin.

"I had breakfast, I got washed and dressed, then I found him," Osborne said. "He was just sitting, staring towards the bed, but I could see immediately he wasn't there. It was just his body. Joe had gone. Then I was downstairs, and the guys were yelling about my hand, and I had to find the words to tell them." He looked down at his left hand. The knuckles were blackened and swollen. "Guess I thumped something. I can't feel it. Can't really feel anything much, right now."

Parnacki watched Venegas jotting notes

for a moment. "Do you know anyone who might have wanted to hurt Joe?"

"A few angry fathers, back in high school. Joe had a way about him. But going steady with Kim changed him completely. He hasn't misbehaved since their first date, eighteen months ago."

"Did you leave your room between 8.15 and 10.00?"

Osborne shook his head slowly.

"Thank you," Parnacki said. "We may have further questions later."

"That was a waste of time," Venegas said, once Osborne was out of the room.

"Not at all," Parnacki replied. "We've got an excellent suspect to start digging into."

Who does Parnacki suspect, and why?

HINT:
SUIT.

SOUTHWELL STOWE

As Christmas approached, Miss Miller found herself once again in charge of arranging the Ornithological Society's festive outing. In the end, she settled on Southwell Stowe, a venue which offered a range of peaceful, bird-friendly habitats on its lands as well as a rather good guest house. She arranged a meal and overnight stay with the couple who ran the guest house, and on the day of their outing the members of the society assembled at the venue shortly after dawn at 8am before spreading out to enjoy their birdwatching.

Although the weather remained persistently cloudy, it never broke into rain or sleet. Miss Miller enjoyed a thoroughly pleasant and successful day, capped off by a spectacularly bright cardinal and a clear sighting of a hoary redpoll, quite a long way out of its usual winter territories. She stayed out until past 4pm, and by the time she made it back, the guest-house was a beacon of light in the glimmering darkness. She celebrated with a hot bath, followed by a fresh pot of tea.

Shortly before it was time to head down for dinner, there was a frantic knocking at her door.

"Come in," she called.

The door flew open. "Oh, thank goodness you're here, Mary."

Isabella Walker was one of the younger members of the group, and prone to excitability. "It's terrible!"

"What's that, my dear?"

"It's Mr. Fonseca. He's been robbed!"

Miss Miller sighed with relief. "That certainly is bad," she said. "What happened?"

"I don't know," Isabella admitted. "Sara asked me to get you. They're in his room."

As it turned out, half the society were in Andrew Fonseca's bedroom. Eventually, Miss Miller managed to get them quietened down, and asked him to tell her what had happened.

"I was indulging in a little snooze," Andrew told her. "I didn't

get back until 4.30. That's a long day for me. I didn't think to latch the door, of course. When I woke up, I discovered my watch and wallet had vanished. They were in my coat when I went to sleep, I'm sure of it. Some dastardly crook must have taken them."

Sara Amos leant in near Miss Miller's ear. "I'm next door. He was snoring like a grampus. Obvious target."

Miss Miller nodded. "Did anybody see anything suspicious? Someone prowling around, maybe?"

Blank stares all round.

"Excuse me," said an unfamiliar male voice behind her. "Mary Miller?"

She turned around to see David, the manager. "That's me," she told him.

"Did I hear correctly that there's been a theft?"

"Unfortunately, yes," she said.

"My dashed wallet!" called Andrew Fonseca.

"I'm so sorry," David said. "What a terrible impression you must have of us. I will contact the police immediately, and while we're waiting for them to arrive I'll question the staff to see if any of them knows something that might help. I'll also order complimentary cocktails to be served to you in the downstairs lounge. I do hope this won't spoil your stay too much. If there's any other way I might be of assistance, please just let me know."

Miss Miller thanked him, and he bustled off.

Ten minutes later, with the group enjoying their drinks, even Isabella Walker had calmed down somewhat. Miss Miller was reflecting on the day when David Southwell appeared at her shoulder again. "One of the maids saw something," he told her.

"Oh?" Miss Miller asked.

"Yes. She was in the dining room with several other girls, preparing it for dinner, when she saw a tall man with a dark complexion walk past, towards the road. She says she didn't think anything of it at the time, given the size of your group."

"That's interesting. Did she get a good look?"

"He had dark hair, and was wearing a red check shirt, a heavy coat, and casual blue trousers. She didn't get a decent look at his face, though, as he was twenty or thirty feet away."

"I see. Are the police coming?"

"They'll have someone up here when they can, yes."

"Excellent. Please have them search her personal effects for the wallet and watch, would you?"

Why does Miss Miller want the witness's effects searched?

HINT:
TIME.

MURDER AT BREAKFAST

Marcus Johns was a tall, gaunt man with thinning hair. He appeared impassive at first glance, but his distress was reflected in the disarray of his clothing—a pajama top, a ratty pink cardigan, pinstriped trousers, and a pair of damply mud-smeared shoes. There was a certain edge to his eyes as well, suggesting that his composure was more external than internal.

"I found Delphine in the kitchen," he told Inspector Parnacki. "I. Uh. I sought help immediately. Then your colleagues arrived, and here we are."

Delphine Johns had been strangled to death, and judging by the pale marks on her fingers, several rings had been removed. The kitchen door was ajar, as was the small gate at the back of the yard.

"Perhaps you could provide me with a little more detail?" Inspector Parnacki kept his voice carefully light and pleasant. "How about earlier?"

"Of course," Johns said. "Well, we got up at about 8am, as usual. While I bathed and shaved, Delphine went downstairs to prepare breakfast. I started to get dressed, and thought I heard her calling me, so I shouted back, but she didn't answer. After maybe half a minute, I went downstairs to see what it was she

wanted. I thought she was going to tell me that we'd run out of eggs again or some such annoyance. I went into the kitchen, and there she was, sprawled by the back door. There might have been a flash of a dark-clad figure at the gate onto the alley behind the yard, but honestly, I'm not sure. It was still raining then, so I couldn't see all that clearly. I froze. It didn't seem to make any sense. I think I expected her to get to her feet and say 'surprise!' or apologize for having startled me. She didn't move, though. I could see that she wasn't breathing. So I got onto the party line, and called for help."

Parnacki nodded. "And what happened after that?"

"I had to get out of that room. I went and sat on the stairs.

Time passed, but I couldn't tell you more than that. Then a doctor arrived, followed by one of your officers. I showed them where the kitchen was. They grasped the problem quite swiftly. More time passed. Then you arrived, and now we're talking. We are talking, yes?"

"We are," said Parnacki.

"I'm glad about that. I wasn't entirely sure. It's been a strange morning."

"Tell me about your wife. Did she have any rivals or enemies, anyone who might want to kill her?"

"Well, no, of course not. I mean, how could she? She was my wife, not some high-powered businessman or shady crook. She grew up in a semi-rural village, and came to the city looking for employment opportunities at the age of eighteen. I met her a few years later, friend of a friend. We married a year later. That was a little more than six years ago. She's a little slow on the uptake sometimes, a bit clumsy, but overall it has been nice. No children so far."

"Did she have hobbies or other interests? What about her friends?"

"Lord, no," Johns said. "Nothing like that. She was a quiet, homey type."

"I see. Just let me check I've got this all clear in my mind. You came out of the bathroom, went downstairs, and found your wife. You went back into the hallway to call for help, and then sat on the stairs until I arrived and brought you here into the lounge. Is that correct?"

"Apart from going to the front door to admit the men who preceded you, yes."

"I'm going to have to ask you to come down to the station with me for further questioning, Mr. Johns."

Johns looked puzzled. "You are? Now?"

"This very instant," Parnacki said, firmly.

Why does Parnacki suspect Johns?

HINT:
CLOTHING.

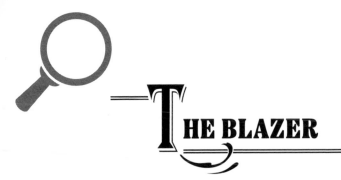

THE BLAZER

Miss Miller was sitting by the riverside, watching a raft of adolescent coots playing with an adult mallard duck. It was a pleasant morning, warm and bright without being stifling, and she had already made a number of interesting observations. Loud, unhappy voices erupted nearby, driving the coots immediately into cover. Putting away her notepad and pencil, she went to see if everything was all right.

A little way upstream, near a bridge, she found a couple engaged in spirited discussion. The man was in his thirties, dressed in casual wear. He looked extremely unhappy. The woman was a little younger, in a long, flowing dress, and appeared more exasperated than anything else.

"I'm telling you, it was right here," the man insisted.

"Good morning," Miss Miller said, approaching. "Mary Miller. Is there anything the matter?"

"Solomon Copeland." The man sounded distracted. "My wife, Clara. My blazer has vanished." He waved towards some trees a few feet away. "It was hanging on a branch. We were only looking at the trout for a few moments. You didn't see … ?"

Miss Miller shook her head. "I'm afraid not, no. No one has

come past me."

"I did tell you not to leave it there," Clara said.

"Darn it," Solomon said. "My wallet was in there." He looked around wildly. "I say, you there, on the bridge."

Miss Miller looked up to the bridge, some fifty feet away, to see a younger man turn to the railing. "Yes?"

"Did anyone come past you in the last couple of minutes?"

The young man thought for a moment. "Actually, yes," he said. "A scruffy-looking fellow burst onto the road from the river bank, struggling to put on his blazer. He bumped into me as he tore past and made me drop my map. It floated under the bridge."

"We'll come on up," Miss Miller called. Looking slightly dubious, the Copelands followed her up to the bridge, where the young man was beginning to look impatient. "My name is Mary Miller, and this is Clara and Solomon Copeland." She looked at the young man expectantly. "Connor Perdue," he told her. "Nice to meet you."

Miss Miller smiled at him. "Could you tell us some more about this scruffy man, Connor?"

"Well, Mrs. Miller—"

"It's Miss, actually."

"Oh. My apologies, Miss Miller. Now … Ah, yes. The man must have been in his mid-to-late thirties. He was tall and lean, rangey you might say. He had dark hair, a little darker than mine, and a patchy beard. Homespun trousers and unhappy-looking shoes, but he was fighting his way into a rather nice navy blazer. Odd, now I think of it."

"That tears it!" Solomon looked fit to begin hopping up and down. "That was mine. He made off with my wallet! Perhaps I can still catch him. Which way did you say he went?"

Miss Miller put one hand on Solomon's shoulder, and the other on Connor's. "Before you go haring off, my dear, perhaps Connor would see the wisdom in owning up and returning your wallet to you? I'm sure the police would take account of such an action."

Why does Miss Miller think Connor is the thief?

HINT:
BRIDGE.

DOUBLE IDENTITY

"I don't see how they got away, Oliver." Kaysen Forrest was a big man with a friendly smile for everybody, usually. Today, he was downright serious—a large sum of cash had been stolen from the office of his seedling and nursery business several days beforehand. "I spotted them at the end of the passageway, near the doors. Okay, it was a bit dark, but I clearly saw a pair of men, under six foot, dressed in company overalls. I could see that the one nearest me was carrying a doctor's medical case. It seemed really strange, so I went after them, and I was through the doors myself in less than thirty seconds. But there was no sign of them at all. The only person out there was Chris Biddle. He heard them run off, but he didn't see anything. The thing is, my stockyard must be a hundred yards wide, and I can see at least another three hundred yards clear. If they'd gone round the side, they'd have run straight into Chris, and besides, there are fences to climb that way. I'd have definitely heard that. No, they just vanished."

Oliver James frowned thoughtfully. "It does sound odd. I don't suppose they could have had a vehicle of some sort?"

Kaysen shook his head. "I don't believe so, no. I can't think of anything both fast and silent enough to get out of my line of sight up the road, let alone without making lots of noise. The police clearly thought I'd gone mad. They took the descriptions, and said they'd pursue all leads, but they didn't seem optimistic. One even pointed out that stolen cash was difficult to recover."

"Well, why don't we try another angle. Who knew you had a decent amount of money on site at the time?"

"I bank on Tuesdays. That weekend was unusually good because those orchids I placed in the Imperial had created a lot of interest. So anyone who was working over the weekend could have guessed—Heather Reeves, Aubrey Fenton, Isaac Brunson, Angelo Delgado, and obviously Chris. But on Tuesday morning, Heather was on the shop floor helping people, Angelo had Monday and Tuesday off, Aubrey was with me in the meeting room we're in, going over the order lists, Isaac was on the tills, and Chris was tidying the stockyard. Besides, even if one of them had tipped off a couple of goons that it was going to be a good day to turn me over, it doesn't explain the vanishing act."

"No," Oliver said. "It doesn't, does it. Still, let's stick with this for a moment. What can you tell me about the staff?"

"Heather's a real sweetheart. She's kind and helpful, no matter how rude or bossy the customers get. She's been here for eighteen months or so. I'll lose her to marriage one of these days, but I won't mind, so long as she's happy. Aubrey has been on board since the start. He's my right hand. I'd be at sea without him. I can't face the idea that he might have betrayed me like that. Isaac is a steady hand, if you know what I mean. Been here three years. A very calm and capable young man. He's awfully sweet on Heather, but he's too shy to chance his arm. I'm thinking maybe I should provide some better chances for nature to take its course there. He'd look after her, that's for sure.

"Chris has worked here for a year or so. He's quiet, but he's got deep waters. Surprisingly knowledgeable about all sorts of topics, on account of his being a bookworm. You'll never catch him without at least something to read. Angelo, finally, has only been working with us for a month or so, but he knows his cultivation like nobody's business. Green thumbs from here to midnight. Get him talking bulbs, and you'll never shut him up. Where does that get us?"

"I'm not sure," Oliver confessed. "How about a look at where these guys vanished?"

"Sure, why not?" Kaysen did his best to summon up a smile, but he was clearly finding it difficult to contain his dismay.

The passage from the meeting room led straight through the building towards the back. It was a long, dimly lit corridor of plastered stone, painted in a leafy shade of green. There were several doors along its length, on both sides. Near the end, the corridor met the hallway which ran from the stock entrance straight along the back to the heated storerooms. The staff restroom doors were opposite the end of the passage, separated by a wide mirror. When they got to the junction, Kaysen pointed right, along the back of the building.

"My office is up there. And that's the stockyard door to the left of the conveniences."

The wide double-doors out into the stockyard were open. Oliver stepped out, and looked around. Kaysen had a point. The yard was a good hundred yards across. It was dotted with saplings mostly, but none of them big enough to hide a man for more than an instant. The trade gate was at the far side, open, with the road beyond it.

"Kaysen," Oliver said finally. "I think I know who did this."

Who does Oliver suspect, and why?

HINT:
PASSAGE.

PRICE'S MISTAKE

There was a good reason, Inspector Parnacki thought, why most wills remained confidential. Benjamin Price had called his family together to inform them of changes he was considering to his will. Specifically, he informed each of them of how much they were due to receive under the current will, and then gave them until the following morning to justify that amount. If he didn't like their answer, he would instead leave their portion to a local charity which looked after homeless cats.

He was dead within ninety minutes, from a potent cocktail of poisons.

The bereaved were still in varying degrees of shock the following morning. Parnacki's first interviewee was Price's business partner, Shane Massey. A few years younger than Price, he had come along to the family meeting at Price's express request.

"I tried to talk Ben out of it," Massey told Parnacki sadly. "But he was determined to put them on the spot. I can't help thinking that if I'd done more … But Ben wanted to see their faces, you see. They didn't know that there was no way to pass the test. He'd already decided to give it all to the cats no matter what. He just wanted to watch them squirm and try to justify themselves, and then rip up the old will in their faces. An unworthy urge perhaps, but he's paid a very high price for it now. He was a good friend to me, and I'll miss him. I stayed at the house until the end of the meeting, but I left immediately afterwards, and went straight to my club. I was there until midnight. Just all a bit too much for me."

Sharon Price was Ben's third wife. Some thirty years his junior, she had taken the events of the previous evening particularly hard. "I just don't understand," she said. "I loved Ben. Why would he do something like this to me? Was it all some sort of peculiar joke? What will happen to me now?"

Inspector Parnacki gradually managed to help her understand that he himself had no answers to any such questions, and got her back to the details of the evening.

"I had no idea what the meeting was about," she said. "Then he dropped his bombshell, and left us to it. I don't think I moved from my seat for so much as a moment until Casey came shouting that Ben was dead. That was a little after nine. Alison, the maid, was there in case we needed anything, and she stayed with me. The others were in and out, apart from Mr. Massey, who was gone almost before Ben finished. Casey kept me company for a while. He's very kind."

Casey Price was Ben's son by his first wife. Just a few years younger than Sharon, he lived in lavish apartments in the city. "Do? I suppose you could say that I'm an art appreciator, Inspector. I have a passion for beauty. Yes, I was taken aback by Father's declaration. He was an odd bird, though, always given to whimsy and calculated cruelty. A bit like those damned cats, I suppose. I significantly doubt that any answer I could produce would have been sufficient for the old coot—except that one, perhaps. Hm? Maybe a little worried, I suppose, yes. I'll probably have to talk to a pal and get set up in business of some sort. A bother. After father's speech, Bianca and I went into the billiards room. We had a bit of a catch-up. The butler was there, I think. Anyway, she wanted to get a snack from the kitchen, so I came back to the library to see how poor Sharon was doing. She's rather lovely, don't you think? Like a porcelain angel. I sat with her for a while, but she was quite out of it. When I went looking for father, I found him quite dead."

Bianca Connors was Casey's full sister. Two years younger than her brother, she was married to the son of a local papermill baron. "He was a nasty old fool," she said. "I never liked him, and I most certainly won't miss him. I'm glad he's dead, in fact. The only time he paid attention to me was when he had just inflicted some emotional hurt or other. It's a shame, though—I was looking forward to telling him that I neither needed nor wanted his money, his time, nor anything else to do with him. Once he'd finished his juvenile stunt and doddered off, I had a bit of a chinwag with Case, in the billiard room. Then I popped down to the kitchen and shared a couple of glasses of sherry with Mrs. Reynolds, the cook. She's always been the sanest person in this dashed madhouse."

Afterwards, Inspector Parnacki went to stroll around the ornamental rose garden, so that he could smoke a pipe and ponder the specifics of the case. He had been there about ten minutes when an officer bustled up with a report. Analysis suggested that Price had ingested the poison some three hours before his death.

Parnacki immediately brightened. "That clears it all up nicely," he said.

Who does Parnacki suspect of being the murderer?

HINT:
TIMING.

THE MINIATURE

"**Y**ou can see what a mess they made, my dear. Obviously, I'm not allowed to touch a thing yet." Lila Palmer frowned at the drawing room. Half a dozen drawers had been taken from three different cabinets, and their contents scattered all over the floor.

"That's terrible," Miss Miller said. "They wanted the Mary Roberts miniature?"

Lila nodded. "There were ten people here last night, all told. I don't want to imagine it of any of them, but any one of them might have crept back in through the patio doors at the side of the house and grabbed it instead of leaving immediately. I'm reasonably confident that we didn't have any intruders during the night after the guests had all departed. The dogs would have started up."

"Maybe you should talk me through the evening, Lila. It might help you to get it straight before the police arrive."

"A good idea," Lila said. "You'd like some tea, I expect."

"Thank you. I certainly would."

A couple of minutes later, furnished with a hot pot of tea, Miss Miller invited her friend to recount the previous evening's events.

"We gathered in the sitting room for a cocktail. From there, we went in for dinner—salmon au hollandaise, neck-fillet of lamb with crisped spinach, and Eton mess. It's such a shame you couldn't come—Mrs. Lea really outdid herself. Anyhow, after dinner, I made sure everyone's glass was fully charged and led them into the drawing room to have a look at the miniature. It was out on the tall side table, the one with the vase of roses. Professor Felton has experience with portrait miniatures, and he was particularly interested that it featured General Oglethorpe. After everyone had taken a good look we stood around chatting for a little while, then I put the piece away and shooed everyone back to the sitting room, where we got into a spirited discussion about Matisse. About an hour after that, people started to leave. When everyone had gone, Wilson and I went up to bed. The maid woke me this morning when she discovered the mess, which would be about six hours ago now."

"Hm," Miss Miller said. "Surely the group was not intact for that entire time?"

"Well no, naturally not. I didn't exactly keep notes on comings and goings, but I remember that Carina Engeld was away for quite some time between the salmon and the lamb. What else? Well, Professor Felton, Justin Choles and Peyton Hatcher were all absent for a short while when we stood after dinner. Reverend Allison left towards the end of the viewing, rejoining us afterwards in the sitting room. Isabella Choles was away for a few minutes during the Matisse conversation. Oh, and Randolph Hatcher spent a good bit of time hunting for Mr. Jessop before leaving, because he wanted to know about the fellow who did the roof repairs last week."

Miss Miller shook her head. "Lila, my dear, it seems to me that there is a fairly clear candidate whom you should convince the police to investigate as a matter of some urgency."

Who does Miss Miller suspect?

HINT:
KNOWLEDGE.

AN INDEPENDENT WOMAN

When police officers forced open Elizabeth Miles's front door at the insistence of concerned friends, they found her dead at the foot of the stairs, her neck broken. Every indication was that she had fallen while descending. She appeared to have been dead since Friday evening, thirty-six hours earlier.

"Parnacki? I've heard of you, haven't I?" Anya Day was Mrs. Miles' part-time cleaner.

"Possibly," Inspector Parnacki told her. "But—"

"Yes, I'm sure I have. You're the one they call Paddington."

"About Mrs. Miles?"

"Oh, yes, of course. Mrs. Miles was very proud and self-reliant. I came in three afternoons a week, Monday, Wednesday and Friday. She was getting a bit frail, but she still kept the house almost completely spotless. There was rarely much for me to do, truth be told, but I think she was grateful for the company. Her children hardly ever came to see her, that's for sure. She seemed fine when I left her on Friday afternoon. How did she die? Nothing too horrible, I hope. She was quite nice—you know, for a wealthy lady."

"It was swift," Parnacki told her, putting on a reassuring tone of voice.

"I'm glad of that at least," Mrs. Day said. "My Reg will be pleased, too. Heard plenty of her stories secondhand, has my Reg."

"Oh?"

"From her youth, as a young, newly married woman in India. I was just telling him the one about her husband and the tigers on Friday evening, actually. Very adventurous, she and her husband were. He must have been a grand sight."

"I see," said Parnacki. "Thank you for your time."

Briony Marley was Elizabeth Miles's daughter. She was in her late thirties, and looked more harassed than upset.

Having made introductions, Inspector Parnacki asked, "Were you close to your mother, Mrs. Marley?"

Marley pulled a face, and sighed. "Not really, Inspector. My mother had many great virtues, and was very popular, but she was a difficult person to grow up with. She never made any great efforts towards my brother or myself. We were palmed off onto a string of nannies and babysitters, and after father died, we hardly saw her at all. She was a little more interested in my children. They'll be sad that their Nana is dead. But she was getting on a bit. It was only a matter of time."

"As it is for us all. Can you think of anyone with a reason to harm your mother?"

Marley looked a little startled at that. "Was she murdered? Your man was quite evasive regarding the cause of Mother's death." She frowned at Parnacki reproachfully.

"I'm just exploring all the possibilities," he said gently.

"I would have thought you could tell that sort of thing from however it was she died," she replied, clearly doubtful. "Still, I'm sure you have to ask. I can't imagine anyone wanting to kill mother, no. She wasn't that sort of woman."

Easton Miles was Elizabeth's other child. A self-described dabbler in assorted business ventures, he was in his early forties. His suit had clearly been expensive when it was purchased, and he carried himself with the sort of arrogant confidence often found in the comfortably well-off.

"It's a terrible turn of events," he told Parnacki. "She was so stubborn. I wanted her to have someone in the house full-time, to help out, but she wouldn't have any of it. Insisted that she was as healthy as a bull. Described the idea as an indignity. I wish I'd pressed harder, now. I'm going to miss her like thunder."

Parnacki nodded. "Were the two of you close?"

"Absolutely. She was a great woman, full of life and fire. The thought of her lying there at the bottom of the stairs, broken— it's almost too much to bear. I always feared that she was going to have a fall. She wasn't getting any steadier on her feet. But she'd as soon stick her head in a crocodile's mouth as use a cane. In fact, I think she did actually do that once. The crocodile thing, that is."

"Do you know if she had any enemies?"

"Enemies? Hardly. One or two jealous hens in her social circle, I dare say. But she was usually most charming, and pleasant with it, rather than spiteful."

Once Easton had departed, Parnacki left the interview and went to find the officer who had discovered the body.

"I need you to go back to the Miles house, Bradley. It's almost certainly a murder scene."

What makes Parnacki think that Elizabeth Miles was murdered?

HINT:
STEADINESS.

THE CLIMBER

"I can't get the sight out of my mind." Carson Long was clearly suffering. "It's been five days, but every time I close my eyes, there's poor Jeffrey, twisted and broken on that pile of rope. It's just so senseless."

Oliver James put his hand on Carson's shoulder. "Give yourself time, Car. You had a terrible shock. How's Hayden bearing up?"

"Worse than I am, to tell you the truth. He was always the strong one of the three of us, too. But I suppose I shouldn't be surprised. He had to watch Jeff fall. At least I was spared that."

Oliver nodded. "It's a mercy. Where were you?"

"I was back in the tent. I never was much of a one for climbing. Not the greatest fan of heights. While Jeff and Hay were off tackling the cliff, I stayed in the tent to catch up on my reading. I heard the screams, and dashed over there. Hay was at the top of the cliff, howling like a demented soul. My mind went utterly blank. I stared at him for a moment or two, and then I looked down and saw Jeff lying there. That's the part that keeps coming back to me. How could there be so much blood?"

"It must have been a horrible sight," Oliver said, then, after a pause, "How were things between the three of you beforehand?"

"Oh, you know, the usual friendly nonsense. The drama about Bella died down a couple of months ago, and things were back to normal. You do know Bella Hall?"

Oliver shook his head.

"She's startlingly beautiful, with a decidedly mischievous streak. Good heart, though. Bags of fun."

"She sounds quite the delight."

"She is," Carson said. "She had all three of us wrapped around her little finger over the summer, playing us off against each other shamelessly. It was all harmless nonsense, and as soon as it started causing some friction, she dropped the games entirely. She must have been soft on Jeff, though. She's almost as devastated as Hay and I."

Oliver nodded thoughtfully. "Please forgive me for asking, but what actually happened to make Jeff fall? Did he miss his footing or something?"

Shaking his head slowly, Carson said, "He was halfway back down. He slipped, and I suppose his anchor gave way. Hay was in no state to give me a detailed account, and I was in no state to hear one. Just that Jeff reached for a tricky hold, and then he was gone. Next thing Hay knew, he was on his knees howling, and I was staring at the bottom of the cliff." He shuddered. "I need a shot of something stiff."

Oliver sighed. "Make it a double, Car. Fetch me one too."

Carson nodded, and poured them both generous drinks. When he handed the glass over, Oliver took it and downed it in one.

"Better get yours under your belt too, my friend. It's about to get worse."

Carson stared at him blankly. "I don't understand."

"Jeff was murdered, Carson. Hayden killed him."

How does Oliver know it was murder?

HINT:
ROPE

MONROE & MONROE

Ethan and Erasmus Monroe were widely known as the best cobblers in the city. They were identical twins, slender, mild-faced men approaching fifty years of age. For years, their only differentiating feature had been the wheelchair that Ethan was restricted to. However, Erasmus's murder had removed any lingering possibility of confusion.

According to the crime-scene reports, Erasmus had been found dead, lying across the floor of the shop workroom, with a heavy impact wound to his left temple. One of his own hammers was on the floor nearby, sticky with blood. It matched the wound. Ethan was on the floor nearby, and had been dragging himself painfully towards his brother when the pair were discovered. He was in considerable distress and disarray, from his wild hair and ripped shirt collar to the scuffed soles of his shoes. His wheelchair had been thrown clear across the room, and it was his desperate screams which had attracted the officer's attention. The shop's cashbox was empty, and the workshop door, which led to the alley alongside the shop, was wide open.

Shaking his head, Inspector Parnacki put the report away, and knocked on the door of the house that the brothers had shared. A gentle-mannered young woman dressed like a nurse answered the door, and showed him through to the room where Ethan was waiting. He thanked her, then introduced himself to Ethan Monroe.

"Thank you, Emily. I wish I could say that it was a pleasure to meet you, Inspector." Ethan managed a weak smile.

"I understand completely," Parnacki replied. "Perhaps you could start by telling me what happened on the day of the murder."

"It was just another normal morning," Ethan said. "I was stitching uppers together. Italian calfskin leather, deep brown, to be made into brogues. Erasmus was nailing boot heels in place, if I remember correctly. Then the bell above the front door went off, so Erasmus put his stuff down and went through into the shop. I heard voices, but I didn't pay any attention until Erasmus shouted. That's when I realized that something was very wrong." He stopped, eyes distant.

"What happened next?

"Two men burst into the workroom. One of them had Erasmus in a head-lock. The other one demanded to know where we kept the money. Then Erasmus groaned horribly. They must have done something to him. I pointed to where we keep the cashbox, and told them to just take it and leave us alone. The one holding Erasmus laughed nastily, while his friend robbed the box. When it was empty, he threw Erasmus to the floor. I was still in shock, and I must have been staring. The one who emptied the box came over to me, yelling something incoherent

about looking at him. Then he tipped me out of my chair onto the floor, and threw the chair across the room. Erasmus howled in rage. I didn't have a good view, but I heard a scuffle, then a horrible crack. Next thing I knew, the men were running out the back. Erasmus was on the floor, and I could see his skull was broken. I started trying to pull myself towards him. I guess I was screaming or something, because a police officer arrived. That's when I learned my brother was dead. Almost ironic."

"How so?"

"Dan Wickline—he's our nearest competitor—has been pressuring us to sell up to him for weeks now. Erasmus was quite tempted, but I flatly refused to even consider it. Now he's dead, I'll have no choice but to sell. I can't manage the business on my own."

"Could Mr. Wickline be involved in this attack?"

Ethan looked perturbed. "No. No, surely not. Dan's

persistent, and a canny businessman, but he's a decent man."

"Very well," Parnacki said. "You said you were pulling yourself along the floor. What, precisely, is the nature of your disablement?"

"I'm paralyzed from the waist down, Inspector. I was thrown from a horse at the age of seventeen. My legs have been dead ever since."

"Can you describe your assailants for me?"

"Of course. One was tall, strong-looking, cheap size nine shoes. His nose had been broken a couple of times. He had craggy features, a wide mouth, and thicky, curly black hair. The other was taller, leanly built, with size tens, quite nice ones. He had little, glittering eyes, hollow cheeks, and a very long, square jaw. They sounded local and ill-educated. I'd definitely recognize them if I saw them again."

"Thank you, Mr. Monroe," Parnacki said. "That's all for now."

As he strolled away from Monroe's house, puffing thoughtfully on his pipe, Inspector Parnacki took another look at both the crime scene report and his interview notes. Suddenly he stopped dead in his tracks. "That changes everything!" he said.

What has made Parnacki suspicious?

HINT:
DAMAGE.

THE MAN IN THE BARREL

'LAND DEVELOPER FOUND DEAD IN BARREL', screamed the newspaper headline. 'Paddington Parnacki on the case!'

Inspector Parnacki sighed and tossed the paper into his waste bin. Muttering to himself about drug-addled ne'er-do-wells, he pushed aside a report into a body found in the river ten days ago and looked over the details from the Costello crime scene. Chase Costello, 52, had indeed been found dead in a barrel hidden in a small dockside shack, having gone

missing some two weeks previously. According to the reporting officer, the victim had an expression of terror frozen on his face.

The death was due to a single stab-wound to the heart, made by a perfectly ordinary kitchen knife, which had been left in the wound. No useful evidence remained on it. There was blood inside the barrel but none around it, and Parnacki felt it safe to assume that the murder had been committed elsewhere.

Costello's wife, son, brother and business partner were all mentioned in the man's will, but as it transpired, there wasn't much for him to leave. Despite his flamboyant and predatory public image, Costello had been close to financial ruin. Almost anyone who'd had financial dealings with the man or his company could have had good reason to want him dead.

Officers had spoken to all the principals. Dessie Costello, his wife, had returned that very morning from a week-long visit to her parents and siblings in her old home town. Aristos Williams, his business partner, had also been out of town for several days on a last-minute trip to try to keep the business from collapsing. Roman Costello, his brother, had been off hunting. Oscar Costello, his son, divided his time between his job and his lady-friend and social life. Olivia Aleman, Oscar's mother, had remarried after splitting up with Chase Costello and was now a housewife who cared for her husband's school-age children from his own former marriage. Luke Aleman, her husband, was a teacher. He was currently abroad with a party of schoolchildren.

Parnacki decided to spend the day talking to everyone in person.

At the victim's large house, the inspector was greeted by Dessie Costello, the widow. She was dressed in black, and seemed reasonably well-composed. According to his notes, she was in her early thirties.

"I want you to find the beast who did this," she told Parnacki. "I loved my husband very much, and this has broken my heart."

Parnacki assured her that he would do everything possible to find the murderer.

"When Chase vanished, I feared the worst. He was never shy about taking the things he wanted, and people get so jealous and spiteful if someone is forthright about being successful. I dare say some of his dealings were a little sharp, but that is the world of business."

"Did your husband mention any threats?"

She shook her head. "Nothing in particular, no. Ari might know more." Her expression softened momentarily, then closed up again. "That's Aristos Williams, Chase's partner," she added quickly. "I don't know him well."

"I see," Parnacki said. "Did you ever hear them talk of such dangers?"

"No. Chase kept business away from home. I only ever met Aristos at functions and the like."

"What about Mr. Costello's family?"

"We weren't close to them. Between you and me, I think they envied him. After the divorce, Oscar was brought up by Olivia, his mother. She tried to turn him against poor Chase. Things became even more difficult for him after we married. Chase's brother, Roman, was just uninterested. They were very different people. I'm afraid that the last couple of weeks have been hard for all of us, though."

Parnacki's next port of call was Olivia Aleman's house. She was in her late forties or early fifties, and lived in a quietly prosperous part of town. Oscar Costello, a shrewd-looking young man, was with her.

"It's a shame that he was killed," Olivia said. "Divorcing me was the best thing Chase ever did, but I'm very sad for Oscar."

"Don't worry," her son said. "It's not that much of a loss."

"Don't talk of your father that way, dear. It's not seemly."

"You didn't see eye to eye," Parnacki said.

Oscar scowled. "He wanted me to be a shark like he was. He always put me down for being too 'weak'. I tried to explain to him again and again that basic human decency and weakness were very different things, but he wouldn't have it. As far as he was concerned, other people were just there to be bulldozed."

Olivia sighed. "There certainly wasn't much gentility to

Chase. He was charming when he was younger, though, and his roguery was somewhat exciting. I got rather carried away. I realized my mistake eventually, and escaped."

"He deserved everything he got with that new floozy of his," Oscar said. "They've been married five years, and she's been carrying on behind his back for at least four of them."

"Oscar!"

"It's true. Several times I've gone round there to find Dad away, and heard her shushing a man, or had her come to the

door all flushed and guilty."

"I see," said Parnacki. "Do either of you know much about his business partner, a Mr. Williams?"

"Aristos? He's a basically decent man," said Olivia. "I always felt that he helped serve as Chase's counterpoint, keeping him from sliding onto the wrong side of the law. I used to see quite a bit of him in the old days."

"I remember him from when I was young," Oscar said. "He was nice to an annoying child."

Parnacki nodded. "And do you see much of your uncle?"

"Uncle Roman, you mean? No, we have very little contact. He vanished as soon as my parents split up. He's a few years younger than my father, and I always rather got the feeling that he only spoke to my mother and me to keep Dad happy. I've seen him maybe twice in the last ten years."

A little later, Inspector Parnacki pulled into the driveway of Roman Costello's lavish home.

"I'm sorry for your loss," Parnacki said to the man, once they were seated in his ornate reception room. "I understand you're a banker."

"Yes," Roman nodded. "I was never sure what Chase saw in land. It's far more efficient to cut out the intermediary and work with money directly. He wanted me to organize him a loan, you know."

"Were you going to do it?"

"I would have tried, of course. He didn't have much

unleveraged collateral, but it could have been possible to sort something out."

Parnacki made a note in his pad. "What can you tell me about Chase's nearest and dearest?"

"There's his wife, Dessie. Chase absolutely adored her. She seems pleasant enough."

"You're not married yourself?"

Roman laughed. "Lord, no. Haven't met the right girl yet. Searching for her is too much fun."

"What about other people close to Chase?"

"Well, he had a rather distant relationship with his son, Oscar. I hardly know my nephew myself—it became hard after his first wife left—but I know that Chase was worried that the boy would never find the backbone to make anything of himself. And there was his business partner, Williams. Charming chap. Bit of a ne'er-do-well, though, I fear."

"Oh? How so?"

"I have it on good authority that he was carrying on with Dessie behind Chase's back."

Parnacki looked at the man sternly. "You didn't tell him?"

"Heavens! Of course not. Chase was hardly known for his fidelity. None of my business."

"I see. Thank you for your time, Mr. Costello."

Aristos Williams met Inspector Parnacki at the offices he had shared with Chase Costello. The man was in his fifties, and neatly dressed. Of all the people Parnacki had spoken to, he seemed the most genuinely saddened.

"I was fond of Chase," Williams said. "He undoubtedly had a ruthless streak, but he was a loyal friend, and very entertaining company."

"Did he have any enemies?" asked Parnacki.

"Oh, most certainly. Few people did deals with him and came off the better for it. There will also be several competitors celebrating this afternoon, I'm sure."

"Do you think one of them might have killed him?"

"In such a byzantine fashion? No, I doubt it."

"What do you know of his family?"

"He was married twice. His first wife, Olivia, was quite nice, but she was his age, so their marriage didn't last. He had a son with her, Oscar. The boy took after his mother. Pleasant, sensitive lad. Chase remarried a few years ago. Dessie is young, beautiful, and I suspect a little bored. He also has a brother, Roman, who he's quite close to."

"And what of yourself?"

"You mean family? I have a wife, a son who seems determined to become a professional astronomer, and three daughters aged between fourteen and twenty-two." He laughed. "Between home and here, I rarely get a moment to myself. I also have a sister who lives a few hours away with her family. We all get together at holidays, either here or there."

"So how would you characterize your marriage?"

Williams paused for a moment, the smile fading from

his face. "You really mean that, don't you? I can't imagine what you've heard, but I adore my wife. I know Chase was a philanderer, but I saw the damage that did first-hand. I'd never inflict that pain on anyone, let alone Maddie."

"Of course," said Parnacki, his voice soothing. "I'm simply trying to get a clear picture."

"All right," said Williams grudgingly.

"What was Chase working on before he vanished?"

"We'd just purchased a large parcel of land near the lake. He intended to build some upmarket homes on it, once he had secured permission."

"I'd like to take a look at that land, if you don't mind," Parnacki said.

"By all means." Williams jotted the address down for him.

When Parnacki found his way to the land, he discovered that it was still lightly forested. The only structure on it was an old wooden cabin. He made straight for it.

Inside, the cabin was surprisingly comfortable. There was a wood-burning stove with an oven and hotplate, a made-up bed, a table with two chairs, and even a wash tub. Several books were on the table, along with two open bottles of beer. One of the chairs was covered with dried blood.

Parnacki permitted himself a short grin. "Gotcha," he said.

Who is the murderer, and how does Parnacki know?

HINTS:

A) *The various testimonies are mutually exclusive.*

B) *Chase's likely time of death is significant.*

C) *Dessie was having an affair.*

D) *Oscar and Aristos were fond of each other, and got on well.*

E) *Chase was not murdered by any of his business enemies.*

F) *Luke Aleman had nothing to do with the crime.*

G) *The case Parnacki was working on before this one is related.*

THE EXAM CHEAT

Miss Miller placed her teacup on its saucer and settled back into her chair. Her cat, Aubrey, leapt from the floor into her lap, and she stroked him absent-mindedly. "If your office has been broken into, Dean, shouldn't you be speaking to the police?"

Dean Harper was the professor of zoology at the university, and a longstanding member of the Ornithological Society. He shook his head wearily. "It wasn't that sort of break-in. They didn't steal anything tangible."

"They stole something intangible?"

To her surprise, he nodded. "Indeed. Every year, I prepare an extra credit paper for my top students to take. It's very hard indeed, and a pass is highly coveted. Only two students have earned distinctions in the past twelve years, and they are both now junior professors. When I discovered the break-in, that was the only thing that had been disturbed."

"When is the exam taking place?"

"Tomorrow. There just isn't time to write a replacement."

"So you want to catch the cheat. But surely there must be—"

"Four, Mary. Just four students are good enough to participate, this year."

"I see," Miss Miller said. "I have to admit, I'm rather intrigued by the idea of this exam. Let's see if we can get to the bottom of your mysterious intruder then, shall we? Hopefully it's one of your candidates, rather than an entrepreneur seeking to make a little money on the side by selling the questions to all of them."

"Good grief, I never even considered that," Dean said. "Do you think it's likely?"

"Honestly, it seems wasteful to try to commodify details of an exam to be sat by just four people, rather than one with a potential purchaser base of a hundred or more."

"That's remarkably cynical of you, Mary."

"Thank you, my dear."

An hour or so later, the pair arrived at the department of biology, where Dean had his office. It was a long, ornately designed brickwork building with attractive flowerbeds along its length.

"Which one's yours?" Miss Miller asked.

Dean pointed out a window, fourth to the right of the large wooden doors. Like all of the windows on the lower floor, it was tall and quite broad. The bottom two-thirds of each window was frosted, to ensure privacy from passersby. The top third, above head height, was hinged to open inwards, to allow a little air. The window frames were painted in a pleasant arboreal green. Burnt orange azaleas bloomed in the flowerbed directly below the window.

"Very nice," said Miss Miller. "Shall we go inside?"

Dean led her into the building, past the departmental secretaries, and along to his office. Once he had unlocked it, she followed him in to find an untidy room crammed with books and papers on every available surface. "You're going to ask me how I know only the special exam was disturbed, aren't you?"

"And you're going to tell me that despite appearances, you know precisely where everything is," she replied.

"Well, not exactly. But I'd know if it had been substantially rearranged, and I genuinely don't think it would be easy to move many of these heaps without having them go everywhere."

"Security through fragility?"

Dean laughed. "Something like that. Anyway, the exam is in this drawer." He opened his desk drawer, and pulled out a roll of paper. "It's been unsealed and untied. Nothing else has. Even if the intruder had taken the time to re-tie other papers—and why would they?—they didn't have access to my seal." He showed her another roll of papers, ornately tied with red ribbon and closed with a seal of white wax. "So they definitely knew what they were going for."

"Yes, I see what you mean. Could any of your students have seen you with the exam?"

"Not in any meaningful way. I only ever work on papers when I'm alone. During the hours that I accept student queries, I keep everything I'm working on rolled up on the sideboard." He indicated a sloppy heap of rolled scrolls of paper to his left. "I'm sure they've all been in over the last couple of weeks, while I was working on the exam, but there would have been no way for them to identify it." He turned, and tapped on the frosted glass of the window. "No peeking over my shoulder, either."

"So do you have any idea how they might have known what to go for? Do you have an assistant?"

"No assistant, and no idea. I was absolutely the only one who knew precisely which exam was which."

"How about happenstance? Say my enterprising exam salesman from earlier broke in, got the wrong exam, but didn't have time to check any others? Your desk drawer would probably be a good place to look."

"The break-in happened some time between my departure last night and my arrival this morning. There are security staff near the door, and they wander the corridors occasionally, but you'd be safe from observation here, in the office. I find it difficult to imagine that someone who went to the trouble to break in would have had just seconds. It takes several minutes at least to copy an exam."

"I can see that there would be plenty of time, particularly with an accomplice. So let's assume that your ambitious student either has the larcenous talents to get into your office while the guard is on his rounds, or acquires a comrade to assist. I assume they all live-in?"

Dean nodded. "Biology third-years are all in Tatum House."

"So their alibis are likely to boil down to having been in bed alone."

"Yes, definitely. Overnight 'guests' are grounds for expulsion."

"Do you have any suspicions?"

"No, I'm afraid not. I wouldn't have thought any of the four would cheat. They're all quite brilliant, and mostly perfectly pleasant."

"I suppose we'll just have to speak to them individually, if possible," Miss Miller said.

They left the office. Dean locked it behind them. "Got to get a better lock," he muttered.

"There are always better locks, but there are also always better thieves. A truly determined and resolved criminal can always get to a prize."

"That's a disturbing thought. Are you saying I should write my exams in code?"

Miss Miller smiled. "If it makes you feel better. Mainly, though, I suggest you improve your security a bit, and just try not to worry about it too much."

Dean shot her a doubtful look. "You're rather unsettling today, Mary."

"I do what I can," she replied cheerfully.

Tatum House was a bland stone cube towards the edge of the university campus that provided accommodation for a little over one hundred and ten students. Dean Harper consulted a scrap of paper, and led the way to the first student's room, on the second floor. "Jacob Walters," he said, when they stopped outside the door. "Very interested in reptiles." He knocked, loudly.

In a few moments, the door flew open to reveal a slim, bespectacled young man of medium height. He was dressed very casually, in a loose shirt and flannel bottoms. He looked at Dean, and his eyes widened. "Professor Harper! I … How can I help? Is everything all right?" He flicked a doubtful look at Miss Miller.

"Good afternoon, Jacob. This is Miss Miller. She'd like to ask you a couple of questions, if she may."

"Of course." Jacob now looked utterly baffled.

Miss Miller beamed at him kindly. "Tell me, Mr. Walters, what does your father do?"

"He's a goldsmith," he said, perplexed.

"Excellent. And where would you say the dividing line lay between reptiles and birds?"

"Archaeopteryx of course, but I really ..."

Still smiling, she poked her head through the open door and glanced around the lad's room, then stepped back. "You have a

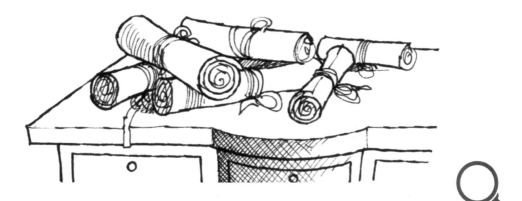

very untidy room, young man. Thank you for your time."

"We must be going," Dean said firmly. "Thank you, Jacob."

"I ..." The young man shook his head, puzzled. "Of course. Good afternoon, Professor." He retreated into his room and closed the door.

Dean gave Miss Miller a very curious look.

"Who's next?" she asked brightly.

Next was Cameron Honeycutt, a zoologist and keen member of the track and field team. He had to stoop to exit his room, and was dressed in a sweater and slacks. Positively skinny, he boasted a large, bushy moustache that didn't quite hide his pronounced overbite, and he nibbled his lower lip when Dean introduced Miss Miller.

"How many children did US President John Tyler father?" she asked him crisply.

"Fifteen," Cameron promptly replied. "Why do you ask?"

"A test of memory," she replied.

"How did I do?"

"Very impressive. Do you happen to have a spare pencil in there?"

Cameron nodded. He vanished into the room then reappeared a moment later with a sharply pristine pencil, which he offered to her.

"No, thank you," she told him. "Good afternoon."

The next student, Nicholas Nagel, lived on the third floor. "Brilliant, but troubled, and prone to drinking," was Dean's evaluation. He knocked sharply on the door.

"Go away," Nagel immediately shouted.

"Nicholas, this is Professor Harper," Dean called.

"I don't care if you're the Pope himself. Leave me alone."

"We just wanted—" Dean began.

"GO. AWAY."

Dean shrugged.

"That's fine. Who's last?" asked Miss Miller.

Alexander Cox lived on the top floor. "He's fascinated by primates," Dean told Miss Miller. "Particularly monkeys. Seems to think they're quite a bit brighter than they've been letting on." He knocked on the door.

A few moments later, a dreamy, overweight young man opened the door. "Professor," he said, without any evident surprise.

"Good afternoon, Alexander. This is Miss Miller. She'd like to ask you a few questions."

"Of course," said Alexander.

"Why monkeys, young man?"

"Monkeys don't pretend," he said, slowly. "They're just what they are."

Miss Miller nodded. "And not apes?"

Alexander shook his head. "No. I don't like apes."

"Thank you for your time," she said.

"Not at all." Alexander nodded to Dean, and closed the door.

As they made their way back down towards the door of

Tatum House, Dean sighed. "Well, I'm going to get a very odd reputation."

"On the contrary," Miss Miller said. "I know exactly who your cheat is."

Who is the cheat?

HINTS:

A) *The intruder knew where to find the exam paper.*

B) *Jacob Walters kept iguanas.*

C) *Cameron Honeycutt particularly enjoyed the long-jump.*

D) *Nicholas Nagel's father died when he was still very young.*

E) *Before deciding on zoology, Alexander Cox had wanted to be an astronomer.*

F) *The intruder had help unlocking and relocking Professor Harper's office.*

G) *The knowledge required to commit the crime came before the intent, rather than after.*

THE GRAND HOTEL

There was something uniquely unpleasant about luxury hotels, Inspector Parnacki thought. A certain bland, over-opulent sameness that tended to leave one feeling somehow outside of reality. Certainly some of the nastiest crimes seemed to take place in such settings. Did the bubble of insulation lead people in this environment to suppose that they were safer from consequence and reprisal? Or was it that long exposure to such languid excess fooled them into thinking that they were somehow lordly? He sighed to himself. It seemed more likely to assume that those who could afford to spend time in such places were somewhat dehumanized compared to the population at large.

Either way, the Grand was a fairly typical example of the species. Thick carpets and lavishly gilded and chromed features were all set off by paintings, statuary, flowers, and frescos. A number of clearly self-impressed guests milled around the lobby, trailing furs and flunkies. Bellhops and busboys darted everywhere, dressed in the staff uniform—a white shirt, shoes and gloves, with a sky-blue jacket and tie, cummerbund, trousers, and a round, brimless drummer-boy cap.

Braden Smallwood had made his money in transport.

Having inherited his father's fortunes and businesses at a comparatively young age, he had turned his attention to rail and shipping. He quickly became one of the wealthy elite of the region through a winning combination of high prices, poor service, and shoddy treatment of his staff. If more workers died in his service than did working for the next four largest of his competitors combined, that apparently was a perfectly comfortable burden to be borne.

He had accrued plenty of aggrieved enemies, but money purchased a lot of protection from the poor, and a lot of forgiveness from the rich. Occasionally some hapless enraged parent, spouse, sibling or child would get close enough to hurl mud or insults, but neither had ever ruffled Smallwood's feathers. Inevitably, the only result would be a lengthy jail sentence for the offender.

Now it seemed as if someone had finally caught up with the man and had spent some time expressing their displeasure with unusual severity. Parnacki made his way through the lobby, shooing off the over-eager bellhops, and proceeded to the second floor.

Smallwood was in Room 16, its doorway flanked by officers. It proved to be a large suite in style with the rest of the hotel. A very large four-poster bed dominated one room, while the second was given over to an ornate yet comfortable reception area, which included two wingback armchairs set near the lively fireplace, a loveseat, and an attractive divan against one wall.

Large windows gave the suite a light, airy feel.

The corpse was in one of the armchairs, naked above the waist. A pair of scissors jutted from one eye socket, but from the mess that had been made of the chest area, they had clearly been used to stab him repeatedly as well. Smallwood's suitcases had been hurriedly searched, the contents scattered around the room. At least one shirt had ended up in the fireplace, going by the remnants of burnt white cuff at the edges of the grate. It was fortunate that a larger fire hadn't started.

Parnacki paced around the suite thoughtfully while he waited for his first interviewee. Apart from the scattered contents of the suitcases and the blood around and beneath the corpse, nothing else appeared to be out of order anywhere. There were no personal items in the bedroom or bathroom, suggesting that Smallwood had only recently arrived. In the reception room, a pot of coffee, a tray of sandwiches and a bowl of fruit jostled for table space with a large bottle of champagne and a pair of glasses.

A knock at the door indicated the arrival of Alison Farris, a wide-eyed maid in her early twenties. Parnacki escorted her to the suite opposite, which the hotel had enthusiastically set aside for his use. Like that of the staff downstairs, her outfit was blue and white, although it looked slightly untidy, and had a large white pinafore over the top of it all.

"I understand you attended to Mr. Smallwood earlier this afternoon," Parnacki said to her, once the introductions were out of the way.

"Yes, sir," Alison said. She was clearly nervous.

"Maybe you could talk me through that." Parnacki smiled kindly.

"Of course, sir."

Parnacki nodded encouragingly.

"Oh! Well, I was told by Lucille that sixteen had a problem with the pillows, and to get myself up here and see what was wrong—oh, Lucille, she's the floor manager for the afternoon shift, and she's got quite the stern reputation, and well-deserved too, so of course I didn't want to do anything what might annoy her, so I came straight over, as you would. So I knocked on the door of sixteen, and he told me to come in, all impatiently, so that's what I did, but not impatiently, obviously, that would be rude and we can't have that, it's really important to make the guests feel at home." She drew in a very deep breath. "So I came into the room, and the guest was there, standing in the doorway between the reception and the bedroom, holding one of the pillows, not like he was cuddling it or anything, but more like it smelled or something, because it was out at arm's length, and he had this offended look on his face. I could see that he hadn't touched his coffee or his sandwiches that he'd made such a fuss over, and sure enough, 'This is filthy', he tells me, and my first thought is to assure him that it most certainly isn't because I put it there myself not two hours ago and I'd never put a dirty pillow out for a guest, but I know I'm never supposed to be arguing with a customer, so of course I just apologize, and tell him I'll replace it immediately, and I'm very sorry, and I can't imagine how it might have got there." Another shuddering breath. "I left the room immediately with the pillow, and of course it was every bit as spotless as I'd thought, but there's no telling with some people, so I went back to the linen room and found a spare pillow and a clean cover, and I put them together, and then I took the replacement back to sixteen, knocking on the door and slipping in. He took it from me, and snorted, then said 'That will do, I suppose', as though I was getting him to sleep on a chunk of sacking or something, so I went back, made the bed up, and got out of there, and that's everything that happened, sir."

Parnacki blinked as she crashed to a halt. "I … see. And how did Mr. Smallwood seem to you?"

"Much like most of the guests, sir. That he'd as soon flay me as kiss me, if you know what I mean."

"I do indeed. What about the suite, did anything seem out of place?"

"Well, now you mention it, I've never liked that marble bust in sixteen, that one of the explorer, there's something just not right about that man's face, it … but I suppose that's not what you mean, sir. No. Everything looked fine inside and out, all spick and span. Apart from the bust. But he always looks like that. So it was all fine."

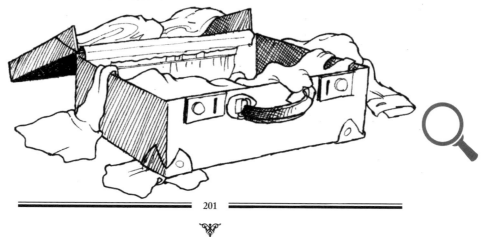

"Thank you, Miss Farris," Parnacki said. "I'll call for you if I have any more questions."

The maid bobbed her head, and rose to leave. "May I say what a pleasure it was meeting you, Inspector, a pleasure indeed. You're a real gentleman, sir. Good afternoon."

Once he was sure that she was gone, Parnacki permitted himself a rueful shake of the head. Sharper than she seemed, Miss Farris was. Many were.

The next interviewee on his list was Damian Edwards, one of the busboys. Edwards was a rigid-looking man in his early thirties, clean-shaven with black hair and a matching black tie. His carriage was rigorously correct, but he tended to fiddle with the hem of his uniform when he was thinking.

"I understand that you discovered the body, Mr. Edwards," Parnacki said.

Edwards jolted slightly. "I did," he said, his voice soft. "It was …"

Parnacki waited patiently.

"Horrible," the man blurted at last. "Obscene. Disgusting. Sorry. This isn't easy."

Nodding, Parnacki said, "And were you making a delivery to the room?"

"No, actually I was refreshing the fruit bowl in eighteen. I heard what sounded like a violent scuffle coming from next door, so I came to investigate. As I approached sixteen, the handle jerked, and the door was wrenched inward. A man raced out and down the hall away from me. I didn't get a good look at his face, but he was wearing a pinstriped suit, and his hands were bloody. I just stopped dead in the middle of the hall and stared. It simply didn't make sense, and I suppose I froze. When I came back to myself, I went to investigate in the room, and that's when I found Mr. Smallwood, all chopped up."

"Can you describe the suspect for me?"

"About five foot ten, and quite muscular, with a short beard and moustache. A pinstripe suit, like I said. Dark brown hair."

"Is there anything else that might help us identify him?"

"Not that I saw, I'm afraid."

"And just to double-check, you didn't disturb anything inside the room, did you?"

"No, of course not. I might have steadied myself against the wall when I saw the body, but I certainly didn't move anything."

"Thank you, Mr. Edwards," Parnacki said. "I'll send for you if I have further questions."

Once he was gone, one of the officers outside Room 16 poked his head into 18, where Parnacki was puffing pensively on his pipe. "Are you ready for the shift supervisor, sir? Lucille Clark?"

"No thank you, Officer Mayhew. I don't think we need to bother her just at this moment. I know who and where the killer is."

Who is the murderer, and how does Parnacki know?

HINTS:

A) *Parnacki was told several lies.*

B) *Consider the movements of the suspects.*

C) *Miss Farris is a little older than she looks.*

D) *The murderer had a very personal grudge against Braden Smallwood.*

E) *Smallwood was not robbed of any valuables.*

F) *This was not the first murder to occur at the Grand.*

G) *Several items of clothing were tossed into the fire.*

WILDHERN

Caroline Heaton was a lovely, graceful young woman with large green eyes and an oddly unflattering haircut. She was also in obvious distress. "It's good of you to see me, Mr. James," she said as she sat down. Her voice was carefully controlled.

"Please, call me Oliver. How can I help? Is Ward all right?"

"My brother is fine, thank you. He sends his best. I think I

might be in trouble, and he suggested that I come to see you."

"I'll do whatever I can, of course," said Oliver. "Why don't you tell me what the problem is?"

"For the last few years, I've been working as a governess for some friends of my father's, Ismael and Ella Calhoun. Do you know them?"

Oliver shook his head. "I don't think so."

"They're lovely," Caroline said. "I've become very fond of their children. Anyway, about three months ago, they took off on a trip to Europe. They expected to be gone for eighteen months, so I started looking for other positions. I didn't have much luck at first, but an advert in the newspaper for a residential position caught my eye. I remember that it specified that duties would be light, but quite varied, and a willing, versatile attitude was a must."

"Do you still have the advert?"

"I'm afraid not. I sent in my letter of application, and shortly afterwards got an interview. That's where I met Mr. Whiting. He's a tall, heavy-set gentleman, and he seemed perfectly pleasant at first. The interview was short and odd, however. He started by specifying that his children were very particular, and told me that I would have to change my hairstyle, and dress in clothes that his wife would provide. I was quite reluctant, but he insisted that my attire would be entirely proper, and was merely to remind his children of a previous, much-loved governess who had passed away. Then he named a very generous sum as a non-refundable advance, and the same again as a fortnightly payment."

"So, of course, you accepted."

"Contingent on there being no impropriety incumbent on the position, yes. I offered Mr. Whiting references, of course. He took them, but he said that he'd like to me start immediately while he was checking them, as his wife was quite overwhelmed without assistance. So I agreed to start work the following morning. This was about two months ago, now."

Oliver nodded thoughtfully. "And were the references ever taken up?"

"Ah. No. As it turns out, they were not. But by the time I found that out, I was already ensconced. The Whitings live in a large house called Wildhern, on the east edge of the city. It's an imposing place, more or less square in the exterior, and three floors tall. The walls are white stone covered with rather fetching vines, and it has a dark slate roof."

"If that's the place I think it is, it has a columned porchway with a rather distinctive checkerboard marble floor, and two different heraldic beasts guarding the main door."

"The lion and the unicorn, yes. So you know that the house is set in a couple of acres of grounds."

"Yes, I do indeed."

Caroline's smile lit up her whole face. "Ward said you'd probably know the place. When I arrived the next morning, Mrs. Whiting hurried me inside, and showed me to a surprisingly large and pleasant room on the second floor. There were a number of clearly personal belongings and keepsakes scattered around that I was told not to touch. The large cupboard inside the room was actually chained shut! I was given the use of a much smaller cupboard inside the bedroom set aside for the maid, Stella. It would have been highly inconvenient, except that every day, Stella set out a fresh outfit for me to wear on the chair at the foot of my bed. I also had to let her give me this haircut. All the staff were under strict instructions never to ascend to the fourth floor of the house under any circumstances. I was quite surprised by how fashionable and informal my outfits were, but Mrs. Whiting assured me that was how her children would most rapidly accept me. She then ordered me not to mention my predecessor again while in the house, so as to avoid upsetting her children."

"That all sounds a little … odd," Oliver said.

"Yes, that's what I thought. I wasn't convinced that any of this was particularly healthy, but the Whitings were being very generous. Subsequent events failed to put me at my ease. I was introduced to the children. Kevin Whiting is thirteen. He has a tutor, Mr. Hall, whom I only ever met in passing. Outside of lessons, Kevin plays the piano or reads, or occasionally roams the grounds hunting butterflies. He manages all these things quite adequately of his own volition, and seems pleasant, if somewhat taciturn. His sister, Emily, is eight, and spends much of the day playing quietly. She also has regular lessons with Mr. Hall, albeit shorter than the ones her brother has. She's a sweet child, and quite chatty with the family, but like her brother, very quiet with the staff."

"Are other staff members well established?"

"An excellent question. I wondered the same thing. Mrs. Stephens, the cook, had been with the family for three weeks when I arrived. There's a young, burly gardener and handyman, Mr. Murray, who preceded me by a fortnight. Stella the maid started on the same day he did. I never got the chance to find out

how long Mr. Hall had been there. Mr. Murray must have been quite the trencherman, for Mrs. Stephens was forever having to prepare trays of food for Mrs. Whiting to whisk out to him."

"Curious," Oliver said.

"Yes," said Caroline. "I asked Stella about the staff's short tenure one evening, and she said that she'd been told that the family had been away for quite some time until recently. I didn't press further, because the peculiarity of my presence swiftly became obvious. The family had a large portrait of the deceased nanny hanging over the stairs, with Kevin and Emily around her. It was quite startling when I first saw it, as she definitely bore some superficial similarities to myself—particularly with my new haircut. It seemed a very odd choice to hang, given all the circumstances. Mr. and Mrs. Whiting were quite unusually tense the majority of the time, and Mrs. Whiting often seemed sad, but the children barely needed any actual looking after. I spent a few hours a day with them, watching them get on with their own lives, but for the most part I was roundly ignored by the entire family. Not in any malicious way, you understand, but it was obvious that I was entirely surplus to requirements. That would have been curious enough, but there were occasions when the routine altered dramatically."

"How so?"

"Well, there were two broad categories of divergence. From time to time, Mrs. Whiting would suddenly be seized by some sort of energetic mood and would round up Stella, the children and me from whatever we happened to be doing. Then she would insist that we immediately engage in sing-alongs at the top of our voices while she played loudly on the piano. Emily was given a surprisingly large drum to bash as well, which she did enthusiastically. These sessions would last anything up to an hour, after which we would all go about our business as if nothing had happened. Mrs. Whiting would invariably be left exhausted by these bursts."

"Poor woman," said Oliver.

Caroline nodded. "On other, rarer occasions, Mr. and Mrs. Whiting would suddenly be filled by some inexplicable bonhomie. In these moods, they became cheerful and gregarious, and insisted that I join the family in some sort of pleasant household activity—telling stories and jokes, or listening to Mrs. Whiting read. There were things for me to entertain myself with, such as half-completed point-work, or a range of novels. I even took meals with the entire family a number of times, with Stella serving me as if I were one of the children. These episodes generally lasted several hours, and were as pleasant as they were inexplicable. They always ended abruptly, with the family returning to their usual attitude of tense withdrawal."

"That is certainly eccentric," Oliver said. "But from what you tell me, you've been with them for two or more months. So I assume that something else has made you feel threatened."

Caroline nodded. "Life at Wildhern was odd and unsettling, but it's only recently that I've felt threatened. About ten days ago, I caught sight of an unfamiliar man in the grounds, trying to hide in a bush not too far from the house. He was tall and powerfully built, and wearing cheap, dark clothing. At a guess, he appeared to be somewhere between twenty-five and thirty. He hadn't shaved for a few days, but it was his expression that really unnerved me. He was staring at me with a kind of … desperation. There's no other way to put it. I told Mr. Whiting, and he flatly insisted I was imagining things. And then he ordered me quite forcefully to utterly ignore any unfamiliar person I thought I might see. He got quite exercised about the matter. It was very odd, even for him. He seemed almost scared."

"You've seen the man again?"

"Six or seven times, yes. He seems to appear when the Whitings are feeling gregarious. He seems utterly fixated on me personally, which is the really alarming aspect. All he does is stare at me, and occasionally mouth some word over and over. It might be 'bag', but I have no idea why. I attempted to ignore him, but his presence is becoming ever more alarming. He has done nothing overtly aggressive so far, but his obsession is clear. I fear it is only a matter of time before something awful happens."

"This is a very peculiar situation."

"I left Wildhern this morning. I tried to resign last night. Mr. Whiting first tried offering me double my current salary, but that just made me more alarmed. Then he flew into a rage, and insisted that I was bound to remain until he gave me leave to depart. I got quite frightened, and agreed, at which point his anger subsided. So this morning, once he was at work and Mrs. Whiting was occupied with Emily, I slipped out. I don't have anything I can take to the police, but I'm terrified the man is going to hunt me down. Ward thought that if anyone would know what to do next, you would."

"You were right to leave the house, I think," Oliver said. "This may be an odd question, but did you ever get the feeling that the house was haunted?"

Caroline blinked. "Why, yes, I did start to wonder. Old houses make plenty of noise, but there would be bouts of persistent and oddly patterned knocks at random moments sometimes, and a few times I also thought I heard faint wailing or weeping. On the one occasion I mentioned it to Mrs. Whiting, she became quite pale. She said it was the water pipes, but she was not convincing, and now I think of it, there did seem to be some notable overlap between the noises starting and the onset of Mrs. Whiting's musical spells."

"I believe I know what has been going on," Oliver said. "You are not in danger, I promise. I will talk to the Whitings tomorrow, and recover any possessions you left when you fled. In return, I ask only that you and Ward come to dinner tomorrow night."

"It would be my delight," Caroline said, smiling. "But what is going on at Wildhern?"

Why was Caroline employed at Wildhern?

HINTS:

A) *The Whitings had no real need of a governess.*

B) *Caroline was never in danger.*

C) *No member of the Whiting family was irrational.*

D) *The gardener, Mr. Murray, also found his duties and instructions hard to fathom, and did not possess an unusual appetite.*

E) *Wildhern was not haunted.*

F) *Caroline was uniquely qualified for the position she was employed to fill.*

G) *The dark man had no interest in Caroline.*

H) *Caroline did not meet the entire Whiting family.*

THE CLUB

The Crockvale Club was one of the city's most popular gentlemen's clubs, and it had a reputation for being firmly on the rakish side. Security had always been tight, but that never prevented the occasional whiff of scandal. All things considered, Inspector Parnacki was not particularly surprised to hear of an attack one Saturday evening, coinciding with the club's annual games weekend.

Christopher Britton was the son of a peer, and one of the leading lights of the Crockvale Club's governing council. He had been found unconscious in one of the rest-room cubicles at 5.30pm. Initial examinations suggested that he had hit his head hard on the wall. Britton's ever-present attaché case was missing, so foul play was highly probable.

Once he arrived at the club, Parnacki's first stop was to speak to Ray Smith, Britton's closest friend on the club council. A tall, bespectacled man in his early fifties, Smith was beside himself with concern. "Christopher is not awake yet," he told Parnacki. "It's been three hours since we found him, and five hours since he was last seen. The doctors seem really worried. They aren't sure if he'll survive this."

"I believe an attaché case was stolen?"

"That's right. He was going to make an award to the winner of the Solo tournament late this evening, so we arranged to receive a rather special prize, a set of gemstones carved into dice. That arrived at 2pm, by secure courier. They may not be in gold settings, but the stones are still very valuable."

"Did anyone else know about it?"

"The competition? Of course. But no one outside the council knew he was getting a delivery."

"What about inside the council?"

Smith looked slightly startled. "Christopher and I had a quick lunch in the bar with some of the other members. We discussed it briefly then. But …" He trailed off.

"Could anyone have overheard you?"

"No. We were quite careful to be discreet."

Parnacki nodded. "I'll need the names of your luncheon partners, then. What were your personal movements over the course of the day?"

"I'll do you a list, of course. Christopher opened the games day this morning at 11am. The entire council came together for that. After that, we split up. There have been a number of different games in play today, so the others have been moving between them. They're all in close proximity to the bar. The plan was to break between 5.30pm and 7pm for a rest and a meal, and then resume in the evening. I helped Christopher take care of some club business after the opening, and then we met up in the bar for lunch between 12.30 and 1.00. I stayed with

Christopher to spend ninety minutes conducting candidate interviews, with a detour at 2pm to receive the samples. At 3.30, I left him to play some Russian whist for a while. That's the last I saw of him." As he spoke, he jotted down a list of names and room numbers. "These are the guest rooms that our people are in, upstairs. I've told them all to stay put."

"Thank you," Inspector Parnacki said. "Please let me know immediately if Mr. Britton wakes up while I'm conducting my interviews."

"Of course."

The first man on the list was Roger Jorgensen, a well-groomed man in his forties with a ready smile and a habit of brushing his hair back with his fingers. "My slot for the first round of the solo was at 2.15."

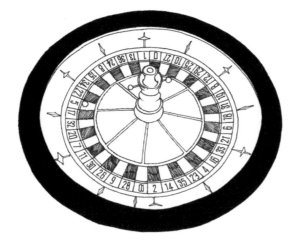

"I'm sorry?" Parnacki replied.

"Oh, my apologies. The club is holding a solo tournament today, in addition to all the other games. All entrants have specific times for their games. We've all been rather concerned about them, as the prize is rather good, and there's a lot of status attached to being the annual champion. Mine was at 2.15pm."

"How did you do?"

"I didn't advance," Jorgensen said.

"Better luck next year, then," Parnacki told him. "What were your other movements today?"

"Well, I tried out the roulette in the morning. That closed in time for me to make it to the bar for lunch with Christopher. Then Elliot and I played liar's dice. I was there for an hour, but he dropped out before me. Wesley took my seat in there, and I admit I popped back to the bar for fifteen minutes for a straightener, just to relax myself for the solo. When that was over, I went on to try my hand at Russian whist. I was in there for an hour and a half, but I left to grab the last half-hour of the blackjack. I went from there to the poker room. Dustin was already there, so when that closed at 5.30, we headed up to our rooms together. That's about it."

Jay Richter was a few years younger than Roger Jorgensen. He was very tidily dressed, and had a somewhat fussy manner. "I spent the morning in the poker room," he told Parnacki. "Elliot was in there with me for the first forty-five minutes, and then he left for his solo slot. After lunch with Christopher, I stayed in the bar with Dustin for half an hour, talking through some problems he's having. He left to join Elliot playing gin rummy, but it was just fifteen minutes until my crack at the solo, so I stayed where I was, talking to Daniel, the bartender. He was working all shift, from opening at noon to the half-five close. I finished the solo in time for the start of the Russian whist, which is quite the challenge, but I only stayed in that for thirty minutes, because the blackjack was beginning. That's my specialty. It ran for two hours, and then I spent half an hour trying hazard. Elliot was in there too. When that finished, I came back to the bar. Wesley met me there, so we had thirty minutes before Daniel closed up."

Dustin Holbrook was in his late twenties, and although his hair and clothes were messy, he seemed pleasant. "I spent my first hour trying out roulette. Roger and Wesley were in there too, but Wes left after half an hour. I got to the bar thirty minutes early, so I could think some things over in peace. I stayed on for a bit after lunch to talk to Jay. After that, Elliott and I spent ninety minutes together playing gin rummy. We left together, and I went on to the poker room. I only stayed there for half an hour, though, because my solo slot was coming up, and I wanted a Scotch beforehand. I got to the bar at half three, and Elliot and Wesley were in there too. Elliot left the bar as I did, at 3.45pm. I went to my solo game, and won! The second round should have started at 7pm, but I don't know what will happen now. Probably have to be cancelled for this year. After the solo, I went back to the poker. Roger joined me there for the last hour, then we came up here."

Elliot Grayson was in his mid-thirties. His short hair and upright posture suggested that he'd served in the forces for a period. "I had an early solo slot. Got the wretched thing out of the way, at least, but I didn't do well. Anyway, I started out with Jay in the poker room. My solo game was forty-five minutes after that. When that was done, I went to the bar. Dustin got there at the same time, but he wanted to do some soul-searching—problems with his sister—so I chatted to the bartender for a time. After lunch with Christopher, I spent half an hour playing liar's dice, and then met Dustin for the last ninety minutes of the gin rummy session. He went off somewhere, and I ended up at the blackjack for half an hour. After a quick fifteen in the bar, I headed to the hazard game, which ran for an hour. There was still thirty minutes from there to the end of play, so I dropped in to catch the end of the Russian whist. Devilish business, that is. I ran into Wesley and Jay leaving the bar, and we came up to our rooms together."

Wesley McDermott was softly spoken and hesitant. "I had rather a whirlwind day, I'm afraid," he told Inspector Parnacki. "When things kicked off 11am, I joined Roger and Dustin in trying out roulette, but only for half an hour. I wanted to catch the first hour of the gin rummy. That took me to lunchtime. I spent an hour in the poker room after that, and then I went for the last thirty minutes of the liar's dice. When the blackjack opened, I spent forty-five minutes playing that, and went from there to the bar. I stayed there for three-quarters of an hour, the middle third of which I spent with Elliot and Dustin, who was about to face his solo game. I went to have a quick look at Russian whist, just fifteen minutes—not for me, I think—and then at the hazard for another thirty. Elliot was in there. That took me up to my own stab at the solo. I crashed horribly, and went to the bar for the last half-hour. Jay was already there. We met up with Elliot as we left, and returned to our rooms together."

Inspector Parnacki was making his way down to the bar when Ray Smith hurried up to him, looking very pale. "The worst possible news, Inspector. Christopher has passed away."

"I'm sorry for your loss," Parnacki told him. "We will pursue every possible avenue to bring his killer to justice. One of your lunch guests did have opportunity to commit the murder, and while we will be focusing our attention on him initially, we will thoroughly investigate all leads."

Who had the time to steal the gems, and when?

HINTS:

A) *The bartender, Daniel, opened the bar at midday, and closed at 5.30pm. He estimated that one or more of the five lunch guests were in there for nearly 60 percent of the day.*

B) *The roulette ran from 11.00 to 12.30.*

C) *The poker room was busy all day, from the 11.00 opening to the 5.30 close.*

D) *The blackjack ran from 2.30 to 4.30.*

E) *The Russian whist ran from 2.00 to 5.30.*

F) *The liar's dice session took place between 12.30 and 2.30.*

G) *The hazard game ran from 4.00 to 5.00.*

H) *The gin rummy session ran from 11.30 to 3.00.*

I) *Games of solo took 15 minutes. Only Dustin won his round.*

DEATH BY FIRE

Inspector Parnacki arrived at the Blake mansion at precisely two minutes past 8pm, according to his pocket watch. When he rang the doorbell, it was swiftly answered by one of his men, to the obvious disapproval of the butler behind him.

"Good evening, Officer Sullivan," Parnacki said, entering the building. "What's the situation here?" He found himself in a large, tasteful entrance hallway, with a crossroads of passageways leading deeper into the house, and a pair of carpeted staircases leading up to the next floor.

"Good evening, sir. The victim is the head of the household, Victor Blake, aged 78. He was found at 5pm by one of his sons. The family doctor, one Atticus Braden, estimates the time of death as a little after 3pm. He was the one who discovered that the old man had been smothered. The family are all here. Everyone is gathered in the sitting room, staff included, with the exception of Perkins here. McNeill is watching them."

The butler stiffened, but stayed silent.

"I'd like to see the crime scene, but I want you here on the door, Officer Sullivan. I'm sure that Perkins will lead the way."

"Very good, sir," the butler said, but he was clearly reluctant.

Parnacki followed the butler up the staircase. "Could you give

me the names of the people who have been in the house today?"
he asked.

After a moment's hesitation, Perkins sighed. "Mr. Blake has
four children, Inspector. Lucas, Benjamin, Delilah and Julian.
All four are currently present. Their families are not. Lucas's
wife, Ramona, and Delilah's husband, Corwin Phillips, took
their respective children home after Mr. Blake was discovered.
Staff here today are the cook, Mrs. Hess, and two maids, Giselle
Renton and Adelaide Morton, in addition to myself. There
are also two visitors, the family doctor, Atticus Braden, and

Mr. Blake's lawyer, Tyrone Bird. There are three police officers present not including yourself, officers Sullivan, McNeill, and Jones. I have deliberately omitted the names of Mr. Blake's grandchildren, as none is over the age of fourteen. Likewise Ian Bates, the groundskeeper, who has not been inside the building today. Mrs. Blake died eight years ago."

"Thank you, Perkins. Very thorough. Was Mr. Blake a good employer?"

"I couldn't possibly comment, sir."

"Of course. If I may ask this instead, then: are you aware of anyone with a grudge against Mr. Blake?"

"No, sir," Perkins said. He looked quite uncomfortable, however. Parnacki said nothing, and after an uncomfortable pause, the man added, "It is commonly accepted wisdom that the presence of a man's lawyer is often an ill omen."

"Indeed it is," Parnacki said. "Anyone could come to the same conclusion."

Perkins gave him a brief grateful smile, and stopped by a heavy door, guarded by a police officer. "Mr. Blake's personal living room is here, sir. I will wait here to take you to the family at your leisure."

"Thank you, Perkins. You've been a great help."

"My pleasure, Inspector."

Parnacki nodded to Officer Jones, opened the door, and went into a comfortable lounge room. A pair of big, felt-covered wingback armchairs were placed either side of a large fireplace well filled with ashes and glowing embers. A poker stood in the empty coal-scuttle. The body of Victor Blake was in the left-hand armchair, legs and lower torso wrapped in a bright wool blanket. Lifting the eyelids, Parnacki immediately confirmed that the victim's eyes were highly bloodshot. The nose and lips were significantly paler than the rest of the face, and there were flecks of blood at the corners of the mouth.

A brief search failed to turn up any likely candidate for the pillow that would have been used to smother the old man. Parnacki looked back thoughtfully at the fire, with its heaps of ash, and from that to Blake's desk, towards the rear of the room. There was nothing obviously out of place on the table and no sign of disarray. Apart from the morning newspaper, there was a pen and ink, a notepad, some blotting paper, a ruler, and a small stack of documents. Parnacki glanced through them, and found only household matters—accounts, grounds maintenance reports, and a clutch of letters of introduction and application.

Ten minutes later, Perkins showed him into the large sitting room. Officer McNeill greeted him, and indicated each of the family, staff, and house guests. As soon as Parnacki introduced himself, Delilah Phillips stood up, clearly annoyed. "How much longer are we going to be kept here?" she snapped. "My children have lost their grandfather today, and they need me."

"I do sympathize," he said. "I just have a few questions. It shouldn't take long. Is there a small room nearby where I could speak to each of you privately?"

Delilah huffed loudly, and sat back down.

"The cubby," Lucas said. "Perkins, would you show the Inspector?"

"This way, sir," Perkins said.

The cubby was a relatively small room with a well-stocked bar and some easy chairs. Parnacki made himself comfortable, and asked Perkins to send Lucas to him.

Lucas Blake was a tall, good-looking man in his early forties. Impeccably dressed, he had an air of easy confidence despite his grave face. "My father was dying, Inspector," he told Parnacki. "Only Delilah and I knew, but he had about six months left. Cancer. If your killer had been a little more patient, he could have saved himself the trouble. Father was irascible, and scared of death, but he was a decent enough man, and a doting grandpa. He rode Ben and Julian harder than Delilah and me—thought it was high time they married. This afternoon? Ramona and I had lunch with Delilah and Corwin. Then we went out for a walk, to keep the children occupied. After a couple of hours of chasing ducks and squirrels, Delilah and Ramona read stories to the little monsters, while Corwin and I played some billiards. When he went back to the ladies, I did a bit of reading. I was just finishing up in there when the shouting started."

Benjamin Blake was a bit shorter than his elder brother, and a little less well presented. He had the same surfeit of confidence, however. "Poor father. I can't imagine who might have wanted him dead. I was the one who found him and raised the alarm, you know. I could see immediately that something was wrong. Still, he had a good run of it. I try to keep out of the house when it's full of nieces and nephews, so I went for a long walk. It was only my and Julian's meeting with Tyrone that kept me from just decamping to my club. He helps the pair of us manage a couple of joint investments. That ran from 3pm to 5pm. I got back from my stroll in time to dash to the meeting.

Then I went to check on father."

Delilah Phillips was clearly irritated, but her mood did not entirely obscure her natural forcefulness or charm. "I suppose Lucas told you about Daddy's illness? I haven't the slightest idea who might have wanted him out of the way. He butted heads with all of my brothers from time to time, but he was never intolerable. It seems somewhat cruel to rob a grandfather of his remaining time with his grandchildren. They're quite distraught, as I'm sure you can imagine. We were with Daddy all morning along with Ramona and her brood. He went up to catch his breath when we sat down for lunch. After that, we took the children out to let them run around for a while, then Ramona and I took turns telling stories. We all know not to pester Daddy when he's resting, but I was starting to get worried about him when Benjamin came to tell us the news. Dr. Braden was here within the hour, and said that the police would have to be involved. That was over two hours ago."

Julian Blake looked tense. The youngest of the siblings, he was only a little past thirty. "I had a meeting with Tyrone Bird, our lawyer," he said. "That started at 3pm. Benjamin arranged it. We spent a couple of hours going over the most minute details about the properties he and I own. Lucas's habits must be rubbing off on him, as he's usually a lot less hands-on. Anyway, Tyrone is on top of it all. Benjamin went up to call on Dad after that, to see if Tyrone could have a word. I wasn't far behind, as I wanted to double-check a detail with him. Benjamin, that is.

He was in Dad's room, staring, wide-eyed. It was dashed hot in there, I'll tell you. Poor Dad. I thought he was indestructible. This morning? What, why?" He hesitated. "I was in my rooms all day until the meeting. Of course I was alone. What are you suggesting?"

Dr. Braden was in his late fifties, a portly man with an impressive moustache. "Victor had cancer. There wasn't much time left. Honestly, he was probably fortunate going out quickly like that—it is not a kind or gentle disease. Yes, I got here around 6pm. Asphyxia was obvious from the eyes and face. Body temperature was close to normal, so he had been dead two, maybe two and a half hours. I'm certain. No, there was nothing in his medical history to suggest natural asphyxiation was likely."

Tyrone Bird was a small, delicate man with large spectacles. "I arrived at the mansion at 2.53pm, at the request of Benjamin Blake. Eight minutes later, I was joined in the cubby room by Benjamin and his brother Julian. We had a discussion about matters private to the two brothers. That lasted two hours and ten minutes precisely. I decided to see if Victor Blake, their father, was available while I was at the mansion, to save me a return journey tomorrow. Benjamin went to check, followed closely by Julian. I then learned that Victor was dead. Tomorrow? Well, I suppose that I can tell you now. He wanted to discuss contingencies on bequests. I don't know any specifics."

Mrs. Hess, the cook, was a tall, strongly built woman with a fierce gaze. "I was in the kitchen. Where else would I be? Yes, all day. Adelaide Morton was in with me much of the afternoon, helping me keep the little ones in tidbits. No, I didn't see anything out of place."

Giselle Renton was one of Blake's maids. She was a willowy nineteen-year-old, with a pale, heart-shaped face. Her hands trembled as she talked, and she kept her eyes downcast. "I was cleaning the house, sir. The whole day, yes. There's a lot to clean. Beds. Cupboards. Mantles. Tables. Wardrobes. No, I didn't see anyone until the afternoon, when the ladies had their reading session for the children. I was cleaning, like I said."

Adelaide Morton was the other maid. A couple of years older than her colleague, she had curly dark hair, and a direct gaze. "I was attending Mr. Lucas and Mrs. Delilah and their families this morning. Didn't see no sign of Giselle. Often don't, these last few months, not when Mr. Julian is around. I'm sure she was busy, though. I went to help Mrs. Hess with lunch, and stayed with her for most of the afternoon, first clearing all the mess up, and then keeping the kiddies fed and watered."

Finally, Parnacki called Perkins back in again. "I was wherever I was needed, sir. I split my time between the various family members. The house was quite quiet between 2.00 and 3.00, which was when I took my own luncheon in the kitchens. Luke and Delilah spent the day with their families. Mr. Blake was with them for the morning. Julian was in his chambers until his meeting. Benjamin left early, again returning for his meeting. Mrs. Hess and Miss Morton were in the kitchens, and Miss

Renton reappeared after the meeting began."

"Thank you, Perkins," the Inspector said. "I think I have everything I need to focus on a prime suspect—and don't worry, I know that this is one occasion where the butler didn't do it."

Who does Parnacki suspect, and why?

HINTS:

A) *Adelaide Morton resented Giselle Renton.*

B) *The groundsman, Ian Bates, would have been able to add some useful testimony.*

C) *The fire in Victor Blake's room was somewhat significant.*

D) *Julian Blake spent the morning and lunchtime in company.*

E) *Not all of the honest testimony Inspector Parnacki received was accurate.*

F) *The killer operated alone, without a co-conspirator.*

 THE LAST RACE

Derby Day was always exciting, but this year it proved unusually tense. The big race was the 1,500 Guinea Stakes, and the talk of the track was Flying Dutchman, a three-year-old colt with a spotless record. His jockey, Liam Cannon, was a rising star in racing circles. He had been a relative unknown until quite recently, but his consistently impressive performances had garnered a lot of interest. He was a famously private man, which merely served to further inflame his legend. Consequently, he got to ride the best horse at the meeting and Flying Dutchman had quickly become the run-away favorite for the race.

Oliver James was as stunned as everyone else at the way the race turned out. Flying Dutchman shot out of the gates into a commanding position and then eased right off. Within a furlong, he had been caught by the third-place pick Oh No, Not Again. Two furlongs more, and Flying Dutchman was at the back of the pack, and stayed there to come in last, while Salome's Private Dance was first past the post, to the sounds of many howls of anguish. Oh No, Not Again and Plato's Dice rounded out the first three.

Most people had assumed that Flying Dutchman had been

hobbled by some injury, although his gait seemed perfectly comfortable. Cannon however gave no explanation, instead throwing his whip savagely at the crowd before storming off the track. Tragically, the young Irishman was found dead a short while later, killed by a bullet to the head. Gossip suggested that he had taken his own life.

Oliver was pondering the odd turn of events when he heard his name. He turned to see Anthony Long, an old friend, approaching him through the crowd.

"Tony! Good to see you," Oliver said.

"You too, Olly. In fact, I rather hoped I'd be able to find you here still."

Oliver arched an eyebrow. "Oh?"

"Something is very, very wrong with all of this. Liam wasn't

a bosom buddy, but I got to know him quite well over the last few months. He rode for my father's stable a few times. He was a good man, and a devout Catholic. He wouldn't have taken his own life, not under any circumstances. We need to work out what's going on."

"Surely the police—"

Tony laughed sarcastically. "If Paddington Parnacki was here, maybe. But he's not, and there's some dunderhead in charge with a chip against the Irish. He's already decided that the world's better off without Liam, and he doesn't much care how it happened. No, it's down to us to show to them that a proper investigation is required. Father's got a lot of clout here, so I have the pull to get us permission to poke around. Particularly now that the police are losing interest, to my mind."

"I see," Oliver said, troubled.

"Are you in? I really need your help."

"Of course I am, old man."

"Capital. First stop is where they found poor Liam, then."

Tony rushed off, and Oliver followed him to a small storage building just behind the raceground's kitchen area. There was a bored police officer standing at the door. He looked up at Tony and Oliver and crossed his arms.

"Strictly no entry, gents," he said, as they approached.

Tony ignored him completely. "This is the place, Olly. It's just a small room in there, with whitewashed walls and floor. I believe that there are some sacks of potatoes inside, or at least there were this morning. That's about it, though. As you can see, this is something of a quiet corner of the ground. Not so quiet that there's any sign of individual footprints in this mud, though."

Nodding, Oliver said "Yes, I see what you mean. Not an unreasonable spot if one did want to kill oneself swiftly." He glanced at Tony's expression. "Not that I'm saying he did, you know? Just that it's a reasonable place for it."

The police officer sighed loudly and theatrically.

"Or for foul play to have happened," Tony said. "Now, follow me."

They moved on from the increasingly disgruntled police officer, round to the kitchen yard. The actual cooking area was inside a large, cheaply built cookhouse which opened out onto a patch of well-churned grass with a gravel path through the middle. Crates and plastic sacks sat out on the ground and people bustled in and out of the kitchens.

"Always crazy here on race days," Tony said. He caught someone's eye through one of the kitchen windows and waved a hand. "Fortunately, I've managed to find out who discovered the body."

A moment later, a cook of around their age hurried out of the door and came over to them, then pulled Tony into the shadow of a stack of boxes. He was a thin man with wispy hair and a determined expression. Tony passed him a small banknote and said "Hello again, Landon. Please tell my friend Oliver what you told me."

The man nodded. "Course, Mr. Long. One of my jobs is to see to the potatoes. I'd done the first two bags this morning, but we were running short, so cook told me to do a third bag. Devils for their mash when it's rainy, punters are. So I went back to fetch a third sack, and there in the middle of the floor was poor Mr. Cannon. For a moment, I just couldn't work it out. I mean, there he was, all neat and shiny, in his racing silks, from the top of his cap to the tip of his boots. Like he was posing for a portrait. But he was lying down, and his head was all at the wrong angle. Then I saw the blood trickling down past the side of his neck. I screamed, I'm not ashamed to say."

"Then you called for the police?" asked Oliver.

"No, sir. They came running, actually. Lots of the lads on the force are fans of the horses, you know. Plenty of them around. They took one look, and dragged me outside to have words. Then it was like a busy coach station in there for a few minutes. He was already cooled off, like the gun, and I'd been in the kitchen until just that minute, so they let me get back to work. Cook was furious, of course. Said I should have grabbed a sack of spuds before shrieking. I'll be paying for that one for a couple of weeks, I don't doubt. It's a real shame about Mr. Cannon, though. Ever so friendly, he was. Usually, he'd have been round before the race for his lucky fruit tart. Never did make it this morning." Landon trailed off, looking sad.

Tony clapped him on the shoulder.

"Just occurred to me," Landon said. "He never will be back for a fruit tart again. Strange, isn't it."

"Did he always come to get something before a race?"

"Most of the time, yes. But not absolutely always. He'd missed once or twice before, when he was nervous about a race. He wasn't as rigid about it as some of the riders are with their little lucky superstitions. I never did meet a jockey who didn't have at least one little superstition, though. Likewise for most owners, to be honest. I suppose they need to feel they've got some control over how things turn out. But that's why I like cooking. It's all in your hands. Bread doesn't go wrong because the flour stumbled halfway through the baking, or because the salt is just having an off-day, if you know what I mean."

"Indeed we do, Landon." Tony smiled at the man. "Thanks for your time. Tell cook my father sends compliments for her lamb this lunchtime."

"That I will, Mr. Long. Bye now." He hurried back over to the cookhouse and vanished inside.

"Interesting," Oliver said.

Tony nodded. "Indeed. There's one more person I want you to chat to." He led them back to the front of the grounds and towards the competitors' area.

A thought struck Oliver as they walked. "Tony, this shock result must have pleased the bookies."

Tony sighed. "They're absolutely delighted, of course. I mean, sure, if you asked any of them, he'd say it was tragic, but the fact is that the bookies make the most money when the favorite loses. When a runaway pick like Flying Dutchman doesn't even place in the top five … well, it's like Christmas for them. You hear about the huge amounts of money won by lucky individuals on crazy results, but it's a drop compared to the vast sums distributed across all the winners on a predictable result."

As they approached a stable block, a young, graceful man in his late teens came over to them. He was wearing a typical stablehand's outfit, with dark trousers close-fitting up to the knee and ballooning out above, a thick white shirt, and a dark vest over the top.

"Ramiro here works for Mason Abraham, Flying Dutchman's owner," Tony said. "This is Oliver James, Ramiro. He's helping me understand Liam's death."

"I'm not sure if anyone can understand it," Ramiro said. "But I'll do what I can."

"You saw Liam last night, is that right?" asked Tony.

"Yes. He was in an absolute rage, storming around the place, muttering about tearing someone a new, uh, hole."

"Any idea what it was about?" Oliver asked.

"A letter. But I've got no clue what was in it. Liam threw it in the fire, and didn't say what was in it. He was still cursing when he left."

Oliver's eyes narrowed in thought. "Did you see him this morning?"

"Sure. He must have been really embarrassed, though. He came in very late, kept away from everyone, and barely managed to mutter an apology to Mr. Abraham for making everyone nervous. None of us saw him again. He didn't even stay with

Dutchman back to the paddock. And then he went and killed himself."

"No," Oliver said. "That he definitely did not."

How can Oliver be so sure? What happened?

HINTS:

A) *Someone wanted Liam to throw the race.*

B) *Flying Dutchman could certainly have won, if he had been allowed to.*

C) *Landon had nothing to do with the murder.*

D) *Mason Abraham lost a lot of money in the race.*

E) *Tony is being completely honest with Oliver throughout.*

F) *It was the blood which finally got the police to take the case seriously.*

G) *The letter Liam received the night before was a warning.*

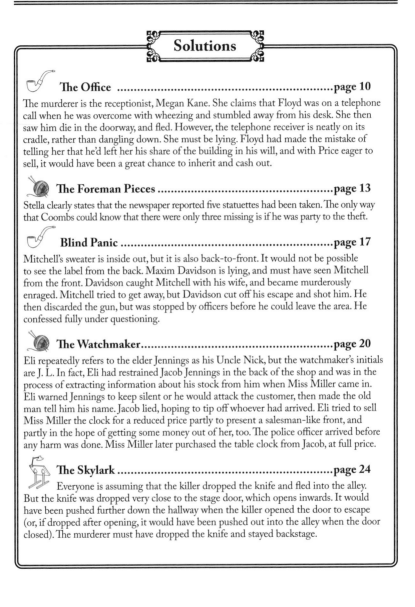

Solutions

The Office ....page 10

The murderer is the receptionist, Megan Kane. She claims that Floyd was on a telephone call when he was overcome with wheezing and stumbled away from his desk. She then saw him die in the doorway, and fled. However, the telephone receiver is neatly on its cradle, rather than dangling down. She must be lying. Floyd had made the mistake of telling her that he'd left her his share of the building in his will, and with Price eager to sell, it would have been a great chance to inherit and cash out.

The Foreman Pieces ....page 13

Stella clearly states that the newspaper reported five statuettes had been taken. The only way that Coombs could know that there were only three missing is if he was party to the theft.

Blind Panic ....page 17

Mitchell's sweater is inside out, but it is also back-to-front. It would not be possible to see the label from the back. Maxim Davidson is lying, and must have seen Mitchell from the front. Davidson caught Mitchell with his wife, and became murderously enraged. Mitchell tried to get away, but Davidson cut off his escape and shot him. He then discarded the gun, but was stopped by officers before he could leave the area. He confessed fully under questioning.

The Watchmaker ....page 20

Eli repeatedly refers to the elder Jennings as his Uncle Nick, but the watchmaker's initials are J. L. In fact, Eli had restrained Jacob Jennings in the back of the shop and was in the process of extracting information about his stock from him when Miss Miller came in. Eli warned Jennings to keep silent or he would attack the customer, then made the old man tell him his name. Jacob lied, hoping to tip off whoever had arrived. Eli tried to sell Miss Miller the clock for a reduced price partly to present a salesman-like front, and partly in the hope of getting some money out of her, too. The police officer arrived before any harm was done. Miss Miller later purchased the table clock from Jacob, at full price.

The Skylark ....page 24

Everyone is assuming that the killer dropped the knife and fled into the alley. But the knife was dropped very close to the stage door, which opens inwards. It would have been pushed further down the hallway when the killer opened the door to escape (or, if dropped after opening, it would have been pushed out into the alley when the door closed). The murderer must have dropped the knife and stayed backstage.

An Unexpected Death .... page 28

David Spencer is supposed to have killed himself by taking twenty or more large pills, yet there is nothing to drink in the room. It's extremely unlikely that anyone would try to dry-swallow that many large pills, and when you consider the fact that his cough would have irritated his throat, the idea becomes implausible. His wife, Sheila, had recently started an affair with another man. She poisoned David, and then staged the scene to make it look like suicide. She got rid of the poisoned beverage, but did not leave a glass of water in its place.

Friday Night Special .... page 31

Toby Black is the murderer. In his testimony, he said that he saw the killer approach Knox from behind, and shoot him in the back. However, the note in Knox's breast pocket had been hit by the bullet, which was later removed from the body, so Knox must have been shot from the front. Black is lying to try to throw the police off the scent.

The Break-in .... page 35

If an intruder had broken a hole in the ceiling and then opened the tarpaulins, the tarpaulins would be on top of the wood, splinters and sawdust, rather than vice versa. Also, if the stack of boxes had been used to escape, the intruder would have been very likely to disturb the detritus on them in the process. In fact, Arlen stole the silver himself and hid it elsewhere, then attempted to stage a plausible break-in scene. Unfortunately, he wasn't very good at it.

The Logician .... page 38

The murderer is Brendon Cotton. The pieces on the large board are in a position impossible to reach according to the rules of chess. A bishop only ever moves on squares of one colour, and each side has one that moves on white squares and one that moves on black ones. On the big board, white's two bishops are just one square apart. That means they both have to be sitting on squares of the same colour. No one who knows how to play chess would make that mistake. Cotton had been embezzling from the client, and Rivera noticed, so Cotton came round to attempt to convince him to help him cover it up. Rivera refused, so Cotton killed him, and then tried to set up a false game. Unfortunately, he made a critical mistake.

The Stolen Statuette ....page 42

There is glass outside the window, but none inside. That means the window had to be broken from inside the house, and Bill was the only one home. He used a larger boot to make the footprints, forgetting also that by treading glass into the prints, he was showing that they came after the breaking of the window. The sad fact is that if he'd asked, Anthony would have given his brother the money to cover his debt.

The Inside Job ....page 45

Emmett Sterling is the thief. He knows that the safe was broken into and that the three clerks are the suspects, even though neither Peter nor Oliver has given him that information. His plan was to drive Peter out of business, and use the ledgers and the money to start up his own firm with Peter's old clients. Unfortunately for him, he was a little too eager to establish his own innocence.

Murder at Mattingley..page 49

The assassin is masquerading as Austin Ball. The gifts that the Ornithology Society members are to present to Kyler Mattingley have received a lot of care and attention. Ball gave a jade statue of a bird similar to the one in Miss Miller's room, wrapped in silk like his handkerchief. It's a peculiar omission, given the importance of the visit and the effort the others have clearly put into their own gifts. The reason for it is that the real Austin Ball has been dead for three days, and the assassin had no idea about a present until Miss Miller mentioned it. The best he could do was wrap an item from his room in his kerchief, and hope it was glossed over until he had escaped.

The Gem Shop ....page 53

Mr. Baldwin was supposedly hit on the head and on the verge of passing out, in a dark room—but he somehow knows that the thief was using a sack made of silk? He has to be lying. In addition, if he had genuinely suffered head-wounds violent enough to render him unconscious for several hours, he would be in the hospital, in a far more serious condition. Baldwin staged the break-in for the insurance payoff, and hoped to pin the guilt on one of his hapless employees.

Victor's Funeral ....page 56

Agatha's ignorance rests on her deafness, but she reacts to the gardener's shout at the same time as Miss Miller. If she can hear a man shout across a busy reception, she can definitely hear a gunshot in the next room—and quite possibly the argument that preceded it.

The Caryatids ....page 61

Although the dates on the statues are perfectly correct by modern reckoning, our year-count didn't come into existence until AD 525. Consequently, it is impossible that a genuine piece could ever be marked as "AD 302" by its maker. At the time, the year was taken from Diocletian's rise to power, and this was the 18th year of the Diocletian Era. Our modern standard of counting years began when a scholarly monk named Dionysius Exiguus, revolted by the idea of taking the date from a famed murderer of Christians, calculated how long it had been since Christ's birth to arrive at the Anno Domini system.

Even so, it didn't become an accepted standard until the beginning of the 9th century.

Deadly Rendezvous ....page 64

The poison was inside the ice-cubes in the pitcher. The bartender, who was in Hansen's pay from the start, had carefully crafted some ice-cubes with poison frozen in the middle. When she ordered the unseasonal iced drink, the bartender used the poisoned ice. Hansen was careful to drink her first glass when it was served, before the ice had a chance to melt, then refilled the glass but left it untouched. That way, she hoped that if any of them came under scrutiny, suspicion would fall on Mrs. Rosenthal, who had not shared in the poisonous drink, and her own survival would be put down to luck.

The Body in the Study ....page 68

The murderer is the maid, Sophie. She claims to have opened the door to the study, seen the Colonel, then slammed the door shut and started screaming. But both the butler and the cook attest that the study was dark, and that the corpse didn't become visible until after the light was turned on. If Sophie didn't enter the room, she couldn't have turned the light off, so it must have been too dark to see anything in there. She knew the body was there because she killed the Colonel, unable to bear any more of his abuse.

The Suicide ....page 71

Natalie Alston's description makes it clear that the tape sealing up the door was on the outside, yet her husband was found dead inside the room. It must have been taped up by someone else, with him inside.

The Miser ....page 74

The maid spread the news that Meyers was killed with a poker, but a weaponized poker is nearly always used as a bludgeoning weapon. Evan Patterson knows that Meyers was stabbed. The only way he could be aware of that detail is if he was the one who committed the crime.

When Parnacki puts even a little weight onto the ladder, it sinks into the snow. If anyone had climbed on it, it would already have sunk to its fullest extent. That means there was no intruder. Only Jackson Stone had the opportunity. He set the ladder up while pretending to go to the bathroom, then "discovered" it, and removed the necklace under the guise of searching upstairs for the thief. Business had been bad for a couple of years, and the sale of such a jewel rarely realizes full value. His intention was to defraud the insurance company for the necklace's face value, and then quietly sell it later for whatever he could get. He steadfastly denied everything, but the necklace was found in the snow the following morning, and nothing further was said about the matter.

Cuevas is supposed to be the captain of the *Emma*, but despite the name, he refers to the ship as "it", rather than "her". This goes against all English-speaking nautical tradition. He's actually a conman, attempting to sucker Cameron into laying down an advance payment for ebony that doesn't exist.

Books are numbered starting from the front side of their first loose page. Pages 69 and 70 are the front and back of the same piece of paper. Whatever the book was, it's impossible for anything to be inserted between those two pages.

Despite at least six cups of coffee being poured, the jug is still full to the brim. Once everyone had gone through to the dining room, Adam quickly slipped the crystal ball into the coffee jug, raising its level up to almost full. He returned the crystal ball a few days later. Alicia didn't mention the orb again, and a month later she had forgotten all about her mystic inclinations.

Matthew Bird is the kidnapper. He knows that Rosalyn cannot identify him by sight and that there is no way she could pick him out of a lineup, so he hopes that her failing to identify him will lift suspicion off him, and if necessary help his case in court.

Last Will and Testament .... page 97

Bob Williams was a longstanding professor of English. Since 'preceding' is one of the hundred most commonly misspelled words in the English language, it is vanishingly unlikely that he would have spelled it incorrectly, with a double 'e', in a document as important as his own will—particularly one inexplicably disinheriting the wife he loved. Someone who wanted to hurt Williams and his family as much as possible had murdered him and written a fake will.

The Missing Murderer .... page 100

There is no murderer. The driver of the truck tried to break into his own safe to steal the contents. Unluckily, the police were very close by. So he kicked open the door to the tailors, fired a few shots out into the empty area of the parking lot and dropped the gun. Then he quickly cuffed himself and hurried towards the back of the room, intending to pretend he had been taken hostage by a robber who had fled. Unfortunately, a police bullet hit and killed him as he was making his way to cover.

Funny Business .... page 103

Obviously, Sabrina would know how Rory took his coffee. But while she checked how Oliver wanted his, she didn't ask Kier. She must have already known, which implies that she is more familiar with Kier than she is even with Oliver, a friend. The truth is that she and Kier had started seeing each other regularly after their meeting at the offices—to plan an extravagant surprise party for Rory's impending 25th birthday.

The Salesman's Wife .... page 107

The spare key is in the stump, but the footsteps only run from the stump to the house. That means the spare could not have been used to open the house, as there would have been no way to replace it. With him being away so much, Chatman became certain that his wife was having an affair—and, in fact, she was. Overcome with jealousy, he decided to kill her. Having booked into a hotel in a nearby town, he sneaked home, put on a larger pair of shoes, and approached the house via the stump to make it look as if the wearer had taken the spare key. Having his own key, he didn't bother actually removing the spare. He went inside, murdered his wife, and in his dazed state afterwards, forgot to fake the return of the key. Then he returned to his hotel in time to clean up and check out early the following morning.

The Narcissist .... page 110

Anthony Stewart knows that Pearce was working on a shipping manifest, despite arriving after the body had been found. Michael Solis attested that Pearce was private about his early-morning paperwork, and the body was slumped onto the desk, with blood over everything. The most likely way that Stewart could know what Pearce had been working on is that he had been the killer. After a short investigation, he confessed. Unable to tolerate Pearce's temper-tantrums and bullying any further, he had come in early and cut the man's throat.

The Cotton Fire .... page 114

Bronze does not cause sparks, so the door roller cannot be to blame. That means Darman is lying. As the police later showed, Darman had set the fire deliberately, having accepted a payment from one of Benjamin's rivals.

The Missing Valuables .... page 118

Ellis claimed to have been in the lodge all evening, but the power there was out that night for nearly an hour. He said that the evening went by in a flash, but if he had actually been in there the power failure would have interrupted the game. The stolen box was later recovered from among his belongings, and he admitted shame-facedly that he'd taken it to cover a gambling debt.

The Cartographer .... page 122

Bruno Marks lied. He said that Chamberlain was at work on a part-completed map, but it is established that the map he was working on had been spoiled earlier in the day, and that he only started a new map when the previous one was complete. As Chamberlain wasn't working, Marks didn't see that he had destroyed the one he'd been working on. Parnacki swiftly discovered that Marks was on the verge of bankruptcy, and needed Chamberlain's financial assistance to stave off disaster. When Chamberlain saw through Marks's attempted con, the men got into a furious argument, and Marks killed him. Confronted with Parnacki's findings, Marks swiftly confessed.

Hendricks in the Frame... page 126

Someone doesn't want the Lawrence development to succeed—but it's not Clayton Hendricks. The building is just a frame at the moment, and from what Clayton says, has been so for more than a week. That makes it easy to see through. But protective tarpaulins were going up as Clayton arrived. With the break room being the other side of the construction from the site office, the builder wouldn't have been able to see the door to the office, let alone correctly identify Clayton entering.

In fact, the builder was planted specifically to hamper progress by the same people who had forced several of the development's suppliers to withdraw. He watched Clayton and the foreman enter the office and leave again, then darted in to steal the plans for his real masters. Clayton seemed an excellent person to blame the theft on, so the builder then found the foreman and told him the fake story. Luckily for Clayton, the builder was so used to being able to see the site office from the break room that he forgot it wouldn't have been visible that afternoon. By the time Clayton and Miss Miller got back to the foreman, the builder had already realized his mistake and vanished.

The Gardener .... page 129

Ian Page's front garden is surrounded by hedges so thick and tall that Parnacki does not see Sam Moody or the policeman until they come through the gate. Yet Moody was able to see every last detail of the supposed suspect from the garden next door. It's clearly impossible. Moody is lying, and what's more, he knows about the murder weapon. Moody has loathed Page for years, ever since a heated disagreement on the boundaries of their respective territories. Page had grown the hedge partly to cast shadow over some of Moody's flowerbeds. Page's recent local award for his own garden had proved the last straw.

Dobson's Leatherworks .... page 132

As Oliver points out, the tannery runoff is pumped into the river, which means the water is full of chemicals devoted to the preservation of organic materials. In that environment, the body would have decayed significantly more slowly than usual, so Kelly's father could have been dead for several days. Eventually, detailed investigation ascertained that Dobson, terrified at the fact that his massive fraud had been uncovered, murdered Kelly's father on Friday evening, then poured a pint of Scotch into him and dumped him in the river, trusting that it would obscure the truth enough for his lawyers to keep him free. It didn't work.

The Bridegroom .... page 135

The suspect is Parker Newman, the bride's brother. The lack of secondary evidence at the murder scene and the position of the body suggest that the murderer took time to clean up after himself. This, in turn, implies that the bloody mark on the wall—left by Gage Osborne's fist, in the shock of grief—is unrelated. Newman would have been unlikely to injure the index finger of his right hand while trying to pin his cravat unless he was left-handed, and while that is certainly possible, 90 percent of the population are right-handed. However, if Newman had arranged the body into the chair, he could quite easily have been pricked by the rose in McNeill's lapel. Following investigation, it turned out that Newman, aware of McNeill's old reputation as a ladies' man, had gone that morning to warn the groom against cheating on his sister. The two got into an argument, and Newman pushed McNeill, who stumbled, fell, and smashed the back of his head into the corner of the heavy windowsill. Panicking that McNeill was dead, Newman staged the corpse in the chair to try to obscure what had happened and cleaned up as well as he could.

 Southwell Stowe .... page 140

At night in the country it's difficult to see anything, let alone from inside a lit room. It would have been very hard indeed for the maid to make out that much detail from that distance, particularly specific clothing. When the police arrived, they found Andrew Fonseca's goods at the bottom of the maid's drawer. She confessed shortly after.

Murder at Breakfast .... page 144

According to Johns' specific testimony, he has remained within the house all morning. However, his shoes are smeared with damp mud, which means he must have been outside, and not on a paved surface. What actually happened was that Johns, a habitually abusive husband, flew into a rage at some imagined slight and throttled his wife to death. When he realized what he had done, he removed his wife's rings and hid them, then went and opened the back gate and left the kitchen door open as well, so that he could try pretending an intruder had been responsible. He made a full confession after Parnacki pointed out a footprint matching his shoes in the fresh mud by the gate.

The Blazer .... page 148

Connor says that he dropped his map, which floated under the bridge. However, as Miss Miller confirms when she first goes to investigate, the bridge is upstream of the Copelands. If Connor had dropped a map, it would have floated down past the Copelands and Miss Miller. In fact, Connor—really named Mason Beck—had noticed that the Copelands were distracted, and grabbed the blazer. He made his way back to the road, extracted the wallet, and dumped the blazer into the river on the far side of the bridge, where it sank. He was trying to make a casual getaway when Solomon's initial shout put him on the spot.

Double Identity .... page 151

Chris Biddle is the thief, and he was acting alone. From the other end of the hallway, Kaysen caught a glimpse of both Chris and his reflection in the mirror at the end of the passage. He thought he was seeing two men, but it was just one. Hearing Kaysen hurry down, Chris quickly hid the stolen briefcase amid the stock, and was going to plead ignorance when Kaysen asked him about a man. Realizing his luck, Chris fed Kaysen's mistaken assumptions, and retrieved the briefcase later. Once Kaysen corrected his witness statement to the police, Chris was investigated, and later confessed. Most of Kaysen's money was recovered.

Price's Mistake .... page 156

All the interviewees have solid alibis for the period after the talk, and none of them have alibis for the time beforehand. But the only person who knew about the change in the will before the meeting was Shane Massey. This means that no one else had a motive to kill Ben at the time when the poisoning took place, so he has to be the murderer. He had been expecting Ben's portion of the company, as per the existing will, but the thought that he would have to share control of the business with a cat charity was too much for him. Once he realized that Ben would not relent, he poisoned him with a slow-onset toxin and made sure he had a strong alibi for the rest of the evening, leaving the members of the family as apparently the only suspects.

The Miniature .... page 160

There's only one person who wouldn't have known precisely which drawer Lila Palmer stored the miniature in—Reverend Allison. Everyone else was in the room at the time she put it away. Given the dangers inherent in snatching the miniature, it's a reasonably safe bet that the thief would not have risked the noise or time involved in emptying out drawers needlessly. The miniature was later found in Reverent Allison's possession. He had been driven to desperate measures by massive gambling debts, and very aggressive debt collectors.

An Independent Woman page163

The precise of cause of death has yet to be released, as evidenced by the testimonies of Anya Day and Briony Marley, but Easton Miles knows that she fell down the stairs. The simplest way for him to know that is if he had actually pushed her himself. Also, his description of his relationship with her clashes with his sister's account. After some investigation, Parnacki discovered that Easton owed significant gambling debts. Confronted with the facts, the man confessed to having murdered his mother for his share of her inheritance.

The Climber .... page 168

Carson describes Jeffrey's body as being on the climbing rope. If Jeffrey had really fallen, the rope would either have come down with him, landing on top of the body, or, if his own attachment to it had failed, it would have stayed in place. Either way, it would not have been all underneath him. Hayden, jealous that his brother had won Bella's attentions, murdered Jeffrey at the top of the cliff, threw the rope off, then dumped the body over.

Monroe & Monroe .... page 171

The crime scene report states that Ethan Monroe's shoe-soles were scuffed. According to his testimony, however, Ethan hadn't taken a single footstep for thirty or more years. If he was tipped from his wheelchair straight to the floor, how would his soles have become scuffed? They wouldn't. Parnacki later had both Monroes carefully examined. The survivor was not Ethan at all, but Erasmus. The man then broke down and confessed. The brothers were being offered a lot of money to sell their business, and Erasmus was desperate to accept and retire. Ethan wouldn't even consider it. The pair got into a bitter argument, ending in Erasmus killing his brother. When he came to his senses, Erasmus immediately saw that his best alibi would be to appear physically incapable of the murder, so he staged the scene and pretended to be Ethan. After a suitable period of mourning, he planned to sell up, move far away, and have a miraculous remission of his disability.

LEVEL 2

The Man in the Barrel .... page 175

Chase Costello was murdered by his brother Roman, but the plan was Dessie's.

When Chase realized that his business was going under, he made sure his life insurance policy was up to date and cooked up a scheme with his wife. Chase pretended to vanish, and went to hide out in the cabin on the land he had just purchased. He then found a hobo of a similar build and age and killed him. He made sure the body was unrecognizable, dressed it in some of his spare clothes and dumped it in the river. The idea was that after Chase had been missing for a few days, Dessie would identify the body as his, claim on the life insurance, and then they'd start a new life together elsewhere.

But Dessie saw the future differently. She and Roman had fallen in love, and Chase's plan provided a perfect opportunity for them to be together. She persuaded Chase to wait a bit longer while she made sure she was beyond suspicion before going to visit her family. Then Roman pretended to go hunting, and instead went to Chase's cabin, spent some time lulling him into a false sense of security, and killed him. He then dumped the body in a barrel at the docks to mislead the police into concentrating on the involvement of organized crime. Roman and Dessie also agreed to make people think she had been having an affair with Aristos, to muddy the waters further.

Roman was eventually convicted of murder, and Dessie of conspiracy. The one silver lining from the whole sad episode was that it brought Oscar and Aristos back together, leading to an enduring friendship.

The Exam Cheat .... page 185

Cameron Honeycutt is the intruder. He's the only one of the students tall enough to be able to see through the top section of the professor's window. In addition to that, he's also the most organized and practical—Jacob is slovenly, Nicholas is absorbed with his own pain, and Alexander is a dreamer—and being good at sports indicates at least some degree of self-discipline. Finally, Cameron has an excellent memory, as suggested by his impressive all-round ability. This would have assisted him in both remembering precisely where the exam was, and in scanning it for cheating purposes.

When confronted about the matter later that afternoon, Cameron confessed. He had seen Dean working on the exam the previous morning while walking past the office, and stayed to observe while Dean put the document away. Then he had recruited a sporting friend with a shady past, and together, they had broken into Dean's office that night. Cameron then opened the exam, and memorized the questions. It was only then that he realized that he could not reseal the roll. He was extremely apologetic, and eventually Dean decided to disqualify him from the exam, but take no further action provided Cameron behaved himself from then on.

The Grand Hotel.. page 195

Damian Edwards is the murderer, and his tie was the main thing that gave him away.

Having heard that Smallwood was in the hotel, Edwards decided to seize the opportunity to avenge his older brother, who died while working for Smallwood. He gained access to the room by pretending to deliver a bottle of complimentary champagne. When he got inside, Edwards quickly took off his jacket and stabbed Smallwood with the scissors he had brought along for that purpose.

Once the man was dead, Edwards realized that his own shirt and tie were covered in blood. He removed them and wiped himself off, throwing the bloody stuff onto the blazing fire. Then he hunted through the man's cases for replacements. He found a white shirt easily, but a black tie was the best he could do. Then he went to call the manager, knowing that if he spoke to the supervisor before everything was thrown into chaos, she would be likely to notice his tie was wrong.

The other major mistake Edwards made was to describe the door being opened by his invented murderer upon exiting—the door handle would have had bloody hand-prints on it if he'd been telling the truth. Also bear in mind that there's no real reason for Edwards to have known the identity of the dead man, and that it's quite unlikely that he would be tasked with checking a fruit-bowl. That would be part of the maid's job when the room was being made up for the day, rather than an errand handed out at random in the afternoon.

Wildhern .... page 205

Caroline was employed solely because of her similarity to the Whitings' eldest daughter, Mary. Some months previous to Caroline's employment, Mr. and Mrs. Whiting discovered that Mary had begun a passionate love affair with a carpenter's apprentice, Dean Kelly. Horrified at such a low-status match, they ordered her to break off the affair. After a series of increasingly bitter arguments and attempts to keep the lovers apart, the Whitings fired all their existing staff and locked Mary in a suite of rooms in the attic. Kevin and Emily were told their sister was very ill, and that they should never speak of her to staff or outsiders in case it caused a disaster.

At first, the Whitings hoped that lack of communication would put Dean Kelly off. When Kelly took to watching the house in his spare time, they hired the closest look-alike they could find—Caroline—and dressed her in Mary's clothes with duties around the house that would make it look as if she was getting on with her life. Mr. Murray was instructed never to apprehend Kelly, but just to inform them if he saw him in the grounds. When so instructed, the Whitings would go to some effort to pretend Caroline was Mary, happily involved in family life.

Other times, when Mary was screaming loudly or banging, Mrs. Whiting would get everyone making as much noise as possible to obscure the sound. Kelly was losing heart when Caroline noticed him. He was too far away to see for certain that she wasn't Mary, but her lack of recognition made him suspicious, and he took to watching her as often as possible.

Shortly after Caroline's departure, the Whitings gave up their attempts to keep Mary segregated. As Oliver pointed out to them, at least they could be sure that Kelly was genuinely devoted to their daughter.

The Club .... page 215

Elliot Grayson had the opportunity. He left the blackjack game at 3.30pm and went to the bar for fifteen minutes, leaving at 3.45, as Dustin did. Elliot then attended the hazard session, which began at 4pm. This means his movements were unaccounted for between 3.45 and 4pm. When faced with the reality of Britton's death, he made a full confession. He had spotted Britton alone in the men's room, crept up behind him, and thumped his head into the wall to knock him out. Then he stole the case and stashed it under a table in a quiet corner of the busy poker room to reclaim later that evening, comfortable that Britton wouldn't be able to identify him. He never intended to cause the man real harm, but, like most people, he didn't realize that an attack serious enough to leave someone unconscious often proves fatal.

Death by Fire .... page 223

The murderer was Victor's son Benjamin. He killed Victor at around 1pm, while Lucas, Delilah and their families were having lunch, and Julian was busy with Giselle Renton. Benjamin's father disapproved of his dissolute lifestyle, and after several arguments, had decided to cut him out of his will so long as he remained unmarried. Benjamin was determined that wouldn't happen. Having left in full sight in the morning, he came back while everyone was distracted. After he smothered his father, he wrapped the body up tightly in a warm blanket, put him in a chair near the fire, and built the fire up with all the available coal as well as the pillow he'd used to smother Victor. Then he sealed the room and left the house again, returning loudly in time for the meeting he had called to give himself an alibi. As Benjamin had planned, Dr. Braden underestimated the time that Victor had been dead, because of the heat in the room and the insulation of the body.

The Last Race .... page 233

The cleanliness of the corpse made Oliver realize that Liam must have been killed before the race. The only way to get in there without getting muddy boots would have been to be carried. It turned out that organized criminals ordered Liam to throw the race, but he persistently refused to do so. After a final warning letter, they killed him the night before the race and kept his body chilled, in a potato sack. A look-alike took Liam's place at the meeting, keeping away from people as much as possible. This replacement threw the race and made his escape. Accomplices then took Liam's body to the potato store-room, took it out of the potato sack and staged it with the gun, and then poured some pig blood as if leaking from the head wound. Unfortunately, they forgot that given the mud outside, Liam ought to have been filthy, rather than spotless. Once the police grudgingly checked the blood and discovered it wasn't human, a proper case was opened, and the murder was eventually traced back to a syndicate of mobsters and crooked bookies.